D1452804

FROM MY SIDE
OF THE BED

Pulling Back the Covers on
Extraterrestrial Contact
A Spouse's Point of View

LISA ROMANEK

Etherean ™
LLC.

Published in the United States by Etherean, LLC, Colorado

Copyright © 2011 Lisa Romanek. All Rights Reserved.

No part of this book may be reproduced in any form or by any electronic or mechanical means, including information and retrieval systems without prior permission from the publisher in writing.

This entire story is true and based on actual events. Some names have been changed to protect individuals' privacy. In some instances, pseudonyms are identified.

First Edition
First Printing: January 2012

Publication Data
Lisa Romanek
From My Side of the Bed

1. ISBN-13: 978-0-9848249-2-2
2. Unidentified Flying Objects – Sightings and Encounters – New Consciousness – United States – Biography

Printed and bound in the United States of America

Acknowledgements

There are so many people to thank and regardless of how many pages it takes, I feel it is important to acknowledge each and every one because without them, I would have been lost—so bear with me. Some people have requested pseudonyms be used but they know who they are...and so do I!

I must first thank my husband, Stan. Thank you for allowing me to be a part of this life-altering journey. If I hadn't met you, I would still be the naïve Nebraska farm girl (even at forty-three) who watched the sky for UFOs, believing that extraterrestrials were real. Now, I know without a doubt that they are! I love you.

A special thank you goes to my children April, Nicole, and Jacob for always loving me unconditionally, even when you thought "mommy" had gone off the deep end. I love you guys with all of my heart.

To my family; my mother, father, sister and brother, and especially my Aunt Jeanne; thank you for believing in me, even if you don't share my beliefs.

To Heidi Soudani, thank you "Honey" for always providing a shoulder to cry on, an ear to whisper in, and a hand to hold. You have taught me patience and grace. You are an angel.

To Heather, for providing guidance, love, understanding, compassion, and many shopping trips when my days seemed darkest. Gar, thank you for allowing and funding the shopping trips, and the many visits when I needed (your wife) my sanity savior the most. You will both forever be in my heart.

Victoria Albright, you came into my life to teach me to let go of fear and jealousy…to trust in love, and to understand that sisterhood is not always due to parentage, but can be a bond created by life's craziest events, including prairie goat sightings .

Rick Nelson, thank you for checking in often, to make sure that I was doing okay, and for reminding me that I am important. Thank you for being a compassionate and fatherly figure to me, Stan, and the kids, as well as a true friend.

Alejandro Rojas, thank you for being the most balanced and calming influence in my life for the past few years. You have taught me to breath deep, open my mind to silence, and accept that reality is….

Richard, thank you for all of your help finding a house—a home, and for making me laugh, when all I wanted to do was cry. Thank you for sharing your enlightenment and knowledge with me. You are a yet unrecognized asset to humanity. Finish your book and share your wisdom!!!

Anna and CJ Locy, thank you for always being there. You are true friends in every sense of the word, and I am blessed to have you both in my life. Sometimes these five words have been my greatest therapy, "Who's ready for a mojito?"

Paola Harris, thank you for encouraging me to speak out for women and to women around the world about my story. Your tenacity for seeking the truth has encouraged me to do the same.

Lucie, thank you for being a friend who could talk about anything and everything that didn't involve UFOs and ETs. You were a lifeline when my life was overwhelmed with everything but the normal day-to-day. Thank you for keeping me grounded!

Mark Stahl, thank you for being there for Stan when his sightings and abductions began, and doing so without fear. No one could ask for a better friend than you...especially on a camping trip.

Ann Romanek, thank you for always being emotionally supportive of not only Stan, but of me and your entire family. You don't hear this enough, so I will write it out for you to read every day. We love and appreciate you, Nani.

Deborah, thank you for being only a phone call away when life threw me an extraterrestrial curveball, and for helping not only Stan, but also me, cope with the information uncovered in the regressions.

Leo Sprinkle, thank you for loving guidance and for conducting the many regressions. Without you, we may never have met "Grandpa," nor acquired the amazing knowledge that he extolled to not only us but through Stan, the world.

Claude Swanson, thank you for helping me to understand that Jake's equation was not just gibberish, though I still have no clue what Bessel functions are, nor do I want to know. Thank you for putting your professional name on the line in support of the truth that we are telling. You can always come home for the holidays.

To Garrison Hardy (pseudonym), for making me write "my story" and not Stan's. From my heart to yours, thank you for everything, especially for introducing me to John.

John (pseudonym), thank you for teaching me to own my power and for helping me to find myself and bestowing on me the understanding of functioning from the heart and only from the heart. You have had a great impact on my life. I will be forever grateful.

Mark and Victoria Leone, thank you for the love, trust, generosity, and acceptance you have bestowed upon my family. I could never in a million years, thank you enough for all you have done for us. Thank you for funding the publishing of this book. May the words contained between these covers make a profound difference in the world.

Brent Smith, thank you for being my final editor, as well as my friend.

Thank you to all of my friends…there are too many to name, who have in one way or another conveyed love and support to me, Stan, and our family. A special thank you to my PRF (Paranormal Research Forum) friends and family, thanks for the many hugs, and for knowing my name is Lisa—not "Stan's wife."

And last, but in no way least, I want to thank my dearest friend, Jenny Smith. Thank you for being you. For making me laugh (everyday) until I nearly peed myself, for yelling with me but never at me, for listening but never judging, for understanding that being a weirdo isn't as bad as people make it out to be. And for having an open mind and heart, and seeing beyond what others want you to see. Regardless of the many miles that now separate us, you will always be my best friend. Love ya!

Table of Contents

Prologue

I jolted awake to a horrible banging at my bedroom window. Someone was yelling my name. I looked at the digital clock on my bedside table and noticed it flashing 12:39. The power must have gone out. The banging started again, and I thought to myself, "What in the world is going on? Stan? Why is my husband outside in the middle of the night yelling and pounding at our window?" I peeked through the blinds to be sure it was really him. With fear gripping at my stomach, I ran to the locked family room doors that opened onto the deck and flung them open. There stood Stan in nothing but his boxer shorts, the frigid Nebraska night air flooding in. As Stan stumbled in, I grabbed his arm and pulled him into the kitchen. He was so cold that he had a pale blue tint to his skin. He seemed to be unable to tell me what had happened and why he had been outside. I looked at the wall clock. Three a.m.? I'm not sure how long the power had been off, but according to my alarm clock, the power had been back on for thirty-nine minutes. I started to rub his arms and back to warm him. He was shaking hard. The more I tried to calm the shaking the more I realized it was more than the cold affecting him. As I rubbed his back, my hand hit a saucer-sized patch of wounds. I said through my tears, "I am sorry, Honey; it's happened again."

My story does not begin here, nor does it end here. This event is just one of many that have happened since that cold November night in 2002, as well as the happenings that transpired in the two years before this unforgettable night. Thousands of women, men, and children share my story—a story of a family struggling with the fear and trauma of alien abduction. It has not been an easy journey. My experiences and those of my husband and family span eleven years and counting, as these incredible events are still occurring in our daily lives. But I want to share with everyone how, in spite of anger, frustration, and fear, we as a family have learned to live with the otherworldly visits.

The purpose of my book is to help twofold. It is to help abductees understand that they are not the only ones who are affected by these seemingly absurd events; their spouses and children suffer right along with them, often times in silence, not knowing what else to do. The main focus of telling my side of the story is to help the spouses of abductees who, like me, feel isolated and alone in a world of forced secrecy. You are not alone—we are not alone. It is normal to be angry, upset, and frustrated. It's okay to have doubts and questions. It's not that you doubt the honesty of the person who is having these experiences, it's just that the situations are so shocking—and at times so bizarre—that you question not only the possibility, but also the plausibility, of the events.

The very idea that extraterrestrial visitors are taking people seems so far-fetched that most people immediately assume that they have lost their minds. But don't worry, you're not insane, and you are not alone. There are people ready and willing to listen and give comfort and support in every state across America—across the world. Unfortunately, many contactees have chosen to remain silent out of fear. Fear of being labeled crazy, fear of ridicule, fear of shame and embarrassment. I, too, was in that position at one time, wanting to hide from the truth, not wanting my family and friends to know what was really going on in my life.

My husband, Stan Romanek, wrote his story of abduction in *Messages: The World's Most Documented Extraterrestrial Contact Story* (Llewellyn Publishing, 2009.) My story fills in the sensitive, heartfelt blanks that he left out. My story is an emotional journey, a trip down a dark, terrifying path of memories that lead to a sunlit field of understanding.

You may come across what you feel are discrepancies between my story and Stan's, but our stories do not conflict. Both versions are accurate in that they serve the memories that we recall independently. My memory tells a story of a family's journey into enlightenment. That story is about what we as a family have felt. What I as a mother and wife have felt. The emotions connected to the abductions, the terror, the heartaches, the anger, the betrayals, the humor, and the love that catapulted us through the most unimaginable events that dominated our lives; and how we managed to overcome the fear and come out on the other end as better people. It portrays how our marriage was tested on many occasions and survived intact through these terribly trying years. In telling my story, dirty little secrets are revealed and truths are exposed. It's not easy to expose one's own faults, to admit that you're not perfect, to lay bare your emotions and thoughts for the world to scrutinize, but…it is liberating.

You may have heard the saying: what doesn't kill you makes you stronger. There is more truth in that statement than anyone could have imagined. Fear won't kill you, but overcoming it will definitely set you free.

A wise man by the name of John shared a bit of wisdom with me, "You can't function from a place of fear. You must always function from the heart—from a place of love and understanding." We have come to realize that love, understanding, and acceptance is all that is needed to move everything in this world into universal harmony. There seemed to have been a wellspring of love that held my family together, a love beyond anything we might have imagined. As long as I could remind myself to let that love flow from my heart, we could get through anything. And, as it turned out, we did.

It's now apparent to me that a voice must speak out for those who feel they are alone in dealing with the alien presence. This is the path that I was put on—that I have chosen. To give of myself— to share my story of enlightenment through love, compassion, acceptance, and understanding for all living beings, human and non-human alike.

1

Weirdos You Meet on the Internet

"What do you mean you saw a UFO?" I asked. "Calm down, Stan." He was talking so fast and so loud I could barely understand what he was saying on the phone.

"It is the craziest thing I have ever seen, I can't believe what I just *frickin'* saw," he said.

"Stan, tell me what's wrong. What are you talking about?" I yelled, in an attempt to calm him down.

"You won't believe me. I'll have to show you. Turn on your webcam, turn on your webcam," he kept repeating over and over again. "This can't be real, this can't be real. I don't believe in this crap." I began to laugh at his state of near hysterics. In his confused and panicked state, he was making little sense.

Via the Internet and the magic of Web cameras, the communication between Colorado and Nebraska was amazingly easy. With the beginning of the new millennium and the end of an unhappy marriage, a new magic was coming into my life. My previous concerns about meeting someone on the Internet had been transformed into an exciting and thrilling freedom I had never known. I married when I was eighteen and had twin daughters by the time I was twenty, and a son at twenty-five. Meeting this man in my thirty-third year was making me feel alive again.

Turning on my computer speakers and microphone, I tested the audio connection through the computer. "Can you hear me, Stan?"

"Yes, I can hear you."

"Okay, I can see you on my computer screen," I said, hanging up the phone. He pushed the play button on his video camera, and there it was on my screen, a UFO. This was the object that had caused all of this excitement. Watching the video gave me goose bumps, and I was suddenly as shaken as he. I stared at the screen. I had never known anyone who had actually witnessed a UFO, or at least anyone who would talk about it. One might understand my shock of actually seeing one firsthand on video.

I first met Stan in the fall of 2000 through an online chat room called "30 Something." Stan and I had a very strong connection from the moment we started talking. He eventually became my best friend—my confidant—my divorce recovery counselor. Now he was telling me he had just seen a UFO. I had been warned about the kind of weirdos you could meet on the Internet. This tale of a UFO was making me wonder if this guy was as normal as he had seemed for the past four months.

As an enticement to get me to come to Colorado, Stan had gone to videotape the mountains and scenery up at a place called Red Rocks in Colorado. He wanted me to know how December in the Rockies takes your breath away with its beauty. Two days after Christmas, on a warm winter morning, Stan set out on what he thought would be a typical excursion to enjoy the fresh mountain air; and that's how a UFO ended up on my computer screen. Across the webcam I could hear him yell, "Do you see it? Can you see the video?"

"Yes, I can see it," I said, focusing intently on the object dancing across my computer screen. As the video tapeplayed, Stan's voice commented on what he was filming.

"Holy crap, what is that thing? Mark, you're going to have a *friggin' canary.*" Mark is Stan's best friend of twenty years, who Stan loved making fun of for believing in UFOs, and had done so for many years. "Where the hell did it go? Whoa, it just shot across the sky. There it is, there it is. I got it on my view screen. Holy crap that thing is weird."

What I was watching on my computer screen was so captivating, I had to watch it a couple of times over. "Oh, my *gawd,* that is amazing," I said. "It's a real UFO."

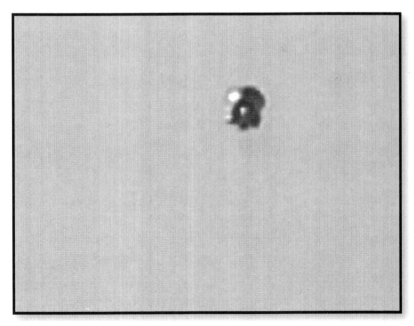

First sighting. Photo taken from video by Stan Romanek.

Stan acted like a kid with a new toy. I love that about him: new things in life can make him so excited. We had never discussed our beliefs in UFOs or aliens, but we had talked about ghosts. There always seemed to be one or two lurking in the corners of my house. I've always been a believer of life elsewhere but, as it turned out, Stan definitely was not a believer. Not even after seeing and recording the UFO.

Watching the object on my screen spurred memories of my childhood UFO watching. My brother and sister and I would get together with our friends to play kickball or some other game, right up until dark. On many nights we would end up lying on our backs, enjoying the feel of the cool grass and other such subtle perks of hot summer nights in Nebraska. Whatever field or the yard we had been playing in that evening was always "the best spot" to search the star-filled sky. Especially after a rousing evening of night-crawler hunting and lightning-bug catching, these adventures made for exciting games we played in the dark. Every shooting star or twinkle in the sky was surely a UFO, at least in my mind. I don't remember having a fear of them. The excitement of possibly seeing alien crafts—something amazing in the night sky—made us feel important. I thought all kids spent their summer nights looking for evidence of alien worlds. I guess not.

Stan mailed me a copy of the tape two days later. The children and I watched it together. It would become a show-and-tell tape for the kids with which to dazzle all their friends. We had never seen anything like it before, and we knew that none of our friends had either. It was a once-in-a-lifetime event, or so we thought.

Sometime during the six months of our new-found friendship, I had fallen in love with this adorable man. Letting my heart lead the way, I decided to finally go to Colorado, to meet Stan in person.

Before leaving Nebraska, I had called my family and friends to let them know that the kids and I were taking a trip, and to let them know when to expect to hear from us. The kids were just as excited as I was to strike out on this grand adventure. We were ready to explore what lay beyond the borders of Nebraska, beyond the stifling confines of our normal day-to-day lives. And to meet the man who had, once again, made me laugh.

Like a scene from a movie, our first face-to-face meeting was magical. We met at a fast-food restaurant, which would impress any redneck girl. Stan was waiting like a nervous school boy. He started walking toward me, and I ran to him. He swung me up into his arms and kissed me. I cannot explain the emotions I felt in that moment. It was like finally finding the other half of me, if that is possible. Stan whispered in my ear, "You are really here." I felt like I had found home in the warm, safe embrace of this man that, until that moment, I had never touched.

I knew my life would never be the same. I knew I would someday marry this man, and that our lives would be full of wild and exciting adventures. But, I had no idea just how right I was, or just how wild those explorations would be.

2

Unfit Mother?

My life felt like a sci-fi/horror/romance novel. With me living in Nebraska and Stan in Colorado, our relationship was based on short visits back and forth and daily phone calls. I hadn't considered what the consequences of being involved with Stan could be, or what life would have in store for us in the future. My daily mantra became: *I love Stan, and that is all that matters.*

Many changes were occurring in my life, some of my choosing and others not. Change is hard for me. It was difficult for me to look inside myself, and to recognize that much of what I saw I didn't like. These changes forced me to confront my fear and to make changes in my life. My self-examination began during the trying times of marital separation, which forced me to leave my fourteen-year career as a Certified Nursing Assistant, and carried on to my eventual divorce. I had no other choice but to start a new life. These challenging times forced me to make changes from who I was to who I wanted to be, whomever that was. I have never thought of myself as anybody special. Actually, I'm very good at believing that I'm nobody special and allowing others to believe it as well. Little did I know life would do the unthinkable to me—holding me up as the image of the "Everywoman!"

After returning home from my Colorado trip, I was feeling on top of the world. Then my life took an unexpected turn for the worse. One afternoon while at work, my boss came to the back of the dry cleaning shop where I was busy pressing shirts. "Lisa, there is a police officer here to see you." *Oh, my gawd, has something happened to one of my kids?* I rushed up to talk to him.

"Are you Lisa?" he asked.

"Yes. What's wrong? Are my kids alright?" I fearfully replied.

"You've been served," he said, handing me an envelope.

"What is this?" I asked.

"You're being sued. It's all explained in the paperwork. I'm sorry. Try to have a nice day," he said as he turned and walked out the door.

Have a nice day? How was that a possibility now? Who would want to sue me? After opening the papers, I began to read the contents. My knees buckled and I almost collapsed to the floor. The shock hit me. Sobbing erupted from within. I could barely stand, let alone walk. My boss helped me to the break area where I tried to regain some semblance of control of my emotions. Unable to speak the words through the tears, I finally shoved the papers at her with uncontrollably shaking hands. As my co-workers gathered around trying to comfort me, I finally unleashed my choked words. "Oh, my *gawd*," I cried. "My ex-husband is suing me for custody. What do I do? I don't have any money to fight him." Shock quickly turned to panic. "I can't lose my kids, I can't lose them. They're all I have."

I kept sobbing as my boss folded the papers and knelt down beside me. As she rubbed my shoulder in an attempt to calm me down, soothingly she said, "We will help you in any way we can. Don't worry. It will work out." I needed to go home, but I was in no shape to drive. As I sat there in near hysteria trying to gather myself, rage began to fill me.

"Who the hell does he think he is? What makes him think I will allow him to take them from me? He has never been there for any of us. Why now? Why is he doing this?" I yelled.

For months, my ex-husband had made my relationship with Stan a constant battle to be fought on nearly a daily basis. He was so consumed with anger that I had met someone so soon after the divorce and that Stan was becoming a part of my and the children's lives. Now he was punishing me. My mind was flooded with angry questions. *How could he be so hurtful to the kids? How could he put them in the middle of such a terrible mess? What makes him think he has a right to mess up the happiness I have found?* Then the answer hit me... I divorced him! It was revenge.

For fourteen years, I had been married to this man and from that relationship I had three wonderful children: April, Nicole, and Jake. My twin daughters were thirteen and my son was eight. They are the light that guides my every action in life. I instill in them that there is no room for prejudice, hate, or dishonesty, and that love is the most important gift you can give or receive.

What rotten timing, I thought. Now I had to deal with the fear of losing custody of my children, financial difficulties, and all of the terrifying things going on in Stan's life as well.

As the weeks passed, the anger continued to grow. *Was being in a relationship with Stan worth all of this turmoil? If I stopped seeing Stan, would my ex-husband stop this whole custody suit? Was I willing to sacrifice the happiness I had found?* These and many other questions weighed upon me.

I was subjected to a three-hour deposition followed by a five-hour courtroom trial. During the deposition my ex-husband and his attorney pulled out all of the stops to make me look like an unfit mother. They posed many questions such as, "Are you taking any medications for illnesses today? Have you had any alcoholic drinks in the last 24 hours? How often do you drink? Do you drink socially, or daily? Do you use any illegal drugs?" I answered the seemingly normal questions, not having a clue what it was leading to. And then they dropped the bomb. "Have you recently been tested for AIDS?"

How in the hell did they get that information? My brain screamed. My medical records were supposed to remain confidential. As the question was asked, I looked across the deposition table at my ex-husband's smirk. He seemed thrilled that he had possibly found something to use against me. Anger exploded in my head. Just looking at him made me want to lunge across the table and slap the smile off his face. After forty-five minutes of objections by my attorney regarding the question, I interrupted, "Yes, I have recently been tested for AIDS." I launched into my explanation, "For the last four years of my marriage, my ex-husband worked seven days a week. He would leave at 5:00 a.m. to go to work, and at times would not come home until 3:00 a.m. the next morning. Maybe he was working that late. Maybe he was having an affair. I felt the decision was a responsible one. I have begun a new relationship with Stan. The test was preformed to make sure that I hadn't inadvertently been exposed to the AIDS virus because of possible indiscretions." After having turned the tables on him, my ex was no longer smiling.

The stress of the constant fighting had begun to take a toll on me. I stopped eating and sleeping. I lost twenty pounds that first month, and was becoming sickly. Normal day-to-day chores were becoming too much for me to handle. I was on the verge of an emotional breakdown.

Never in my life had I been exposed to the overwhelming power of shame. It is a force that cripples and devours you, sucking the very essence of life from your soul. Confronting this shame became my first awakening. I discovered an indestructible part of me that I had never known existed.

When we finally went to trial, the attorneys asked about Stan's background and his family. My ex's lawyer launched implications about my sexual activities with Stan and anyone else since the divorce. She grilled me about the dangers of meeting someone over the Internet. My ex-husband's attorney insinuated that my mental stability should be questioned because I had not been afraid that Stan could kill me and the kids. I didn't know whether to laugh or cry at the accusations. I explained that I had no fear of Stan and neither did any of my friends who had met him. He was a nice guy. Stan and I were like the many thousands of people that met on the Internet, started a friendship, and fell in love. Why should I be made to feel ashamed of that? As protective as I am with my kids, the accusation of exposing them to anything harmful struck me as ridiculous. And my ex-husband knew it. How could my relationship with Stan be construed to mean I was an unfit mom?

This legal confrontation forced me to take a long hard look at myself. The introspection forced me to evaluate my role as a mother. It was through this self-analysis that I have come to realize that a good mom is a good role model. She is the person she hopes her daughter will become and the kind of woman she hopes her son will marry. She has unshakable integrity, strength when she needs it, more strength when demands are made, and kindness at the root of her being. Mothers make mistakes, of course—we are human just like everyone else, though through the eyes of our children, we appear superhuman. We need to remember to acknowledge our mistakes and try to rectify them. I have always taken my responsibility to my children seriously, and have provided structure to my children's lives even as a married-single parent. Teaching them right from wrong in a world full of hatred, prejudices, and dishonesty wasn't always easy. My kids have always felt adored, valuable, safe, and secure. These very simple traits I have instilled in them are the very qualities that helped create the well-adjusted, independent, capable, young adults that they have become, and no court of law was going to tell me otherwise.

It is important for the people who are struggling with divorce and custody issues to know that we all go through tough times in our lives, some more heart-wrenching than others. There is no way of knowing what the future will bring, and it is useless to live in the past. What I learned from my trials was to be true to who I am and to remain optimistic and thankful.

All of the details of my personal life were being made public knowledge. I didn't like being questioned and criticized for my decisions. I wanted vengeance for the slanderous remarks that were made against me. My friends, family, my ex-husband, and the judge, made me feel ashamed and worthless; it tore at me. I actually began to feel ashamed of all of my actions because of outside sources telling me that I should. I began to believe the lies swirling around me. But what I refused to believe was that I wasn't caring for my children! Apparently, the Judge didn't believe it either. I retained custody of my kids.

Shame is defined in the Encarta Dictionary as "a painful emotion caused by a strong sense of guilt, embarrassment, unworthiness, disgrace, dishonor or condemnation." Shame is a powerful emotion that causes you to question yourself. It is put upon us by others and by societal teachings at a very young age. Shame is not a stranger to the individuals who are abducted, as I would later discover. Societal condemnation, like what I experienced around the custody suit, would prepare me for the unbelievable events about to unfold.

By the time the trial finally ended, I had begun to listen to what my ex-husband wasn't saying instead of what he was. I began to understand that he was trying to hold on to me in some way, and the kids as well. He had been trying to force Stan out of our lives so that things could remain the way they had been for the past fourteen years—dysfunctional, yet familiar. By my ex-husband's forcing this custody suit, he was trying to make me choose between him and Stan, and was punishing me for leaving him to begin with. In that moment, the hatred I had been feeling towards him changed into understanding. My shame unmasked itself. It was as if a light switch had been thrown on and suddenly I could see. I was ashamed of my behavior, my actions towards my ex-husband, the lack of understanding I had given him. My shame came from allowing anger to rule my decision-making and my actions. I had to find the courage to admit not only to myself but to others that this was a necessary lesson, a lesson in change. I now understood at least one lesson that I was supposed to learn from this experience. Winston Churchill once said, "Courage is what it takes to stand up and speak; courage is also what it takes to sit down and listen."

The indestructible part of me surfaced, and with clarity I realized I am powerful, not powerless. I am important to many people because of who I am—I am a mother.

Stan's UFO experiences remained a secret throughout the custody battle. Had they come to light, I'm sure all hell would have broke loose and the information would have been used not only to try to prove me unfit for exposing my children to such preposterous ideas, but also mentally unstable for my belief in extraterrestrial life.

This legal battle was the catalyst for my own self-reflection, a mirror through which I faced my inner demons and came out a different person. Little did I know of what still laid ahead of me. This legal battle would also prove to prepare me for even greater challenges and would demand even more courage and conviction in the not-so-far-off future.

3

Abductions Begin

Stan invited me to join him and his best friend, Mark, on a road-trip to Pennsylvania. Excitement overcame me. My worldly travels had been limited to Nebraska, Kansas, Iowa, Missouri, and most recently Colorado. A road trip was just what I needed to wash away the remaining stress of the custody suit. My spirits needed renewing. Even though I knew the trip wouldn't be all fun, I was thrilled to embark on this new adventure.

On the second day of our trip, as we entered Pennsylvania, I noticed an object that looked out of place in the afternoon sky. "Look, up there on the left, by that little puffy cloud. Do you see that shiny thing up there? What is that? Is that a UFO?" Mark and Stan were frantically scanning the sky to locate the object at which I was pointing.[1]

"Oh, my *gawd*, I think it is a UFO," Stan said. Mark was also searching the sky, but couldn't spot what appeared to be a small craft hovering and sparkling in the bright sunlit sky. Less than a

---

[1] Stan Romanek, *Messages: the World's Most Documented Extraterrestrial Contact Story* (Minnesota: Llewellyn Publications, 2009), 23

minute had passed and the object remained motionless. It suddenly zipped across the sky to the south before coming to a halt again. This time Mark got a quick glimpse of it but still couldn't see it well enough to have an opinion as to what it might be.

"Did you get a good look at it? What did it look like, Lisa?" Mark asked.

"I did," I stammered excitedly. "It looked like a silver disk, like those in sci-fi movies from the '70s." I was overwhelmed with excitement at possibly having just witnessed my first UFO.

A few days later, as we were traveling back home, I noticed another object in the sky. It looked like the same object I had seen before. *That can't be another UFO. There is no way on God's green earth that I could see another one.* I suddenly remembered that we had binoculars under the seat. As my eyes focused on the object, there was no room left in my mind for doubt. What I was looking at was indeed a UFO. It was a typical saucer, again like the ones you see in the old movies. I couldn't believe my luck. In my excitement, I climbed all over the back portion of the van trying to get a better look at the craft.[2] Mark scrambled to get his video camera. His excitement of personally seeing and documenting a UFO made him act as giddy as a boy at a county fair. The dramatics began as Mark rolled down his window and jostled haphazardly in the front seat trying to securely position himself. Pulling one foot up underneath his other leg, creating a tripod effect for balance, he leaned as far out of the window as he could. As unbelievable as it would seem, Stan was trying to accomplish basically the same maneuver while in the driver's seat. We were driving 80-85 miles per hour down the interstate with two seemingly insane men hanging their heads out the windows. Then it became more like heads, arms, and as much

---

[2] Romanek, *Messages*, 24

as their upper bodies as they could manage without falling out or wrecking the van.

My excitement of seeing a UFO was quickly turned to fear. I was more afraid of swerving into other traffic than of the UFO. Every time we tried to pull over to the side of the road, the object would disappear behind a puffy cloud and be gone, only to come out again after we started driving. Hours of this reckless chase wore on my nerves. When I couldn't take the fear of crashing anymore, I begged the guys to pull over at a rest area. To my relief it was the last we saw of the object.

As we returned to the van after using the rest stop facilities and browsing the gift shop, Mark and Stan scanned the sky, looking for the UFO again. They were having a hushed conversation about me.

"Lisa is really mad, I think she might be mad enough to try to poke a fork in our heads," Stan said. I didn't know if Stan was teasing or really trying to scare Mark.

"I hope not. What did we do to make her so mad?" Mark queried.

"I don't know. Why don't you let me drive for awhile and you take a nap," Stan told Mark. As I listened to the conversation between the two of them, I began laughing silently.

They're both idiots. Where in the hell does Stan come up with this crap? Poor Mark, he looks terrified. I wasn't about to let them know that I found their conversation humorous, so I continued to glare at them.

"No, I'll drive and you go back there with her and take a nap. I'm not stupid," Mark replied. It seemed they were arguing about who got to drive at that point to avoid falling asleep, making themselves easy targets for their shared fear that if one of them were to fall asleep, he would fall victim to Stan's concocted fork-in-the-head theory. I just rolled my eyes at them. *Men can be such drama queens.* I should have made a point of sneaking a fork or two from the restaurant when we stopped for lunch, and displayed them on the dashboard. Neither of them would have slept for days.

After the many hours of adrenaline pumping—UFO chasing, crazy driving, and manic conversations—we were all exhausted. The spacecraft didn't return. I personally was glad that the damn thing had finally found something else to do. The guys, however, were disappointed and suddenly became obnoxious. Whether it was from boredom or their frustration at me for making them stop at the rest area, I didn't know, nor did I care. We were all ready to get home. I missed my kids and was sick of being trapped in a car with Stan and Mark.

On September 20, 2001, a week after returning from our trip to Pennsylvania, I was home in Nebraska and Stan was back to work in Colorado. He had worked a twelve-hour shift that day at the bicycle shop that he managed. Stan called me when he arrived home from work, very upset.

I answered the phone, "Hello?"

"Hi, Baby," he said.

"Hi, Honey, how was your day?" I asked.

"It…it was interesting, something really weird happened. I really don't want to tell you. I don't want you to think I'm crazy."

"Why would I think you're crazy? Just tell me what happened."

"Okay. Well, the last customers had just left the shop and I was locking up for the night, when one of the men who had just left ran back in to get me. The guy excitedly told me that there was this huge red flashing object over the store. I raced outside to see what the man was talking about. It really was the weirdest thing I had ever seen. It was a pulsing red object that looked like a giant soccer ball, with a blue light dangling, or shining, from the underbelly of the craft."

"Do you think it was another UFO?" I questioned.

"Yes…I do. Do you think I'm crazy?" he asked.

"Absolutely, you are nuttier than a fruitcake," I teased him, trying to lighten his mood.

"Well, it gets worse," he interrupted.

"Honey, how could it get worse? If that thing was another UFO, it's the third one you have seen in the past year. Why do they seem to be showing up all of the time?"

"Trust me, it gets worse. I ran back into the shop, finished locking up for the night, and ran to my car. I was not comfortable being alone after what I had just seen. I tore out of the parking lot and headed for home. I was feeling safer knowing that there were other people on the streets. Then I saw it. The same red blinking soccer ball thing was hovering in the distant sky. All I could think was to drive faster, and hope that it would go away. It didn't. The object seemed to close the distance of the miles between us in only a few seconds. I could see it as clearly as I had when it was above the shop. It followed me to the apartment."

"It followed you home?" I asked incredulously. "Why would it follow you home?"

"If you don't believe me, you can ask Mark or my sister. They were waiting at the apartment for me, so we could go out to dinner. They saw it, too."

"I'm not saying I don't believe you, I am trying to understand why it followed you."

"I think I'm going to go to bed. I have a terrible sick headache, in the back of my head. I don't know if I will be able to sleep but I need to lie down. If I can't sleep can I call you back?"

"Of course you can," I said. "You know I am always here if you need me." As I hung up the phone my thoughts were running rampant. This was becoming a habit, his calling me with these wild UFO tales. True or not, it didn't make sense why all of a sudden he was seeing so many of them, or why this one had followed him home. I had a hard time sleeping that night. I was worried about Stan and what possible reason there could be for his seeing all of these crafts. *Maybe its karma,* I thought. *Maybe it's a karmic payback, for picking on Mark for all of those years. Karma can be a mischievous thing. It can bite you in the butt when you least expect it.* Who better to teach this lesson to than the very person who had been so mean to other people for their belief in UFOs?

The next morning Stan called complaining that he had sores around his wrists, ankles, and his lower back. Flipping on my web camera, "Stan," I said, "Go to your computer, and show me. My webcam is already on." The hair on his wrists had been rubbed off. Stan was desperately trying to come up with a reason for the injuries.

"What do you think caused these sores?" he asked me.

"I think you should strip your bed. Maybe you have a spider in your bed, and it's not real happy about sharing," I replied. That was the best reason for the sores that I could come up with. My intuition was telling me that something was bothering him besides possible spider bites. I asked, "Stan is something else bothering you?"

"No! I am just tired," Stan snapped. "I have to go, but I'll call you later. Bye."

He called again a short time later to tell me about what he called a "crazy dream."[3] Stan hesitantly explained, "I had a really bizarre dream about three aliens coming to the apartment during the night. They kind of looked like people, but they had long faces, and *hmmmm*, like possum people." I kind of chuckled because I thought he was teasing me.

"Maybe you had such a weird dream because you saw another UFO last night," I suggested. Stan became so emotionally upset that he broke down and cried, which made me feel horrible. I was so far away from him and couldn't help him. Something seemed to be terribly wrong.

As Stan struggled to get control of his emotions, he admitted, "I don't know if it was a dream. I remember feeling the female alien touching me. I remember grabbing one of the two males and trying to throw him off the balcony. It seemed so real, but that's crazy, it couldn't have been real. Aliens don't exist. Do they? I'm so confused!"

How could my boyfriend go from being the smart, strong, funny, sweet guy that I met a year earlier to this babbling, bawling, confused man that I was now listening to? I had found the man of my dreams. I had fallen in love, I wanted to get married, and live happily ever after. But what if he was delusional? I have always been a caregiver. Taking care of people was my job, and working with the elderly, my passion. But this was out of my realm of understanding. I was totally unequipped to deal with alien abductions.

Should I tell him it was only a dream and try to convince him that the spider-in-the-bed story was the only logical explanation? Who could I call for help? As my mind cleared, I realized no one would believe me. They would question Stan's sanity, and mine. If I called a

---

[3] Romanek, *Messages*, 34

doctor, told him that my boyfriend thought he had been abducted by aliens, and asked him to help Stan, he would think I was crazy. I didn't want anyone to think I was crazy. I did the only thing I knew how to do. I listened and reassured him. I loved him, what else could I do?

Conversations with other experiencers have taught me that a common emotion shared among people who have alien contact is denial. They want the experience to be something that their minds have created, instead of a possible reality. Many abductees have a fear of being ridiculed for believing they have experienced something extraterrestrial. This pales in comparison to the fear of being labeled crazy. It seems that many abductees remain silent for this reason. Just like Stan, the contactees don't want their partners to shun them. They don't want their spouses or partners to be afraid or ashamed to be with them. They hold the details of their experiences secret, inside themselves, and try to deal with them alone.

Many couples have difficulties stemming from this behavior, especially when the abductee has endured, as many do, the trauma of the sexually-oriented experiences which cause shame, fear, guilt, and confusion. Many experiencers like Stan remember the ETs taking sperm or ovum, which in Stan's case was a very painful procedure. Post-Traumatic Stress Disorder (PTSD) has been found in many claiming to have had these experiences. That is a lot for a spouse to understand, especially when they don't know the cause of this behavior. I am glad Stan shared his experiences with me. Even though I worried for his safety, I was able to support him through this and help to alleviate some of his turmoil. I let him know I loved him and supported him no matter what. Thank God I had friends to talk to about this. I sat listening to Stan's story, spellbound.

"Stan, do you think it was a dream?" I asked him.

"Of course it was a dream, what else could it have been," he snapped. "There are no such things as aliens."

Mark suggested that Stan contact an organization called MUFON (Mutual UFO Network). MUFON agreed to help Stan because of his UFO sighting in December, and now this possible abduction nearly a year later. They assigned an investigator to the case. The investigator, who I will call Gio, started his investigation by taking photos of the wounds on Stan's body, making sure things were documented thoroughly.

After months of dwelling on what had happened, Stan and Gio talked about regression. Hypnotic regression therapy refers to using the hypnotic state to access memories that might otherwise not be accessible. The subconscious human mind is like a computer, it stores data. The hidden folders collect traumatic experiences that the conscious mind is not ready to deal with. They agreed that they would talk with a hypnotherapist named Deborah Lindemann. Deborah is a board certified clinical hypnotherapist, and has a private hypnotherapy practice in Fort Collins, Colorado. She is the founder of the Center for Extraordinary Explorations, which is dedicated to extraordinary experiences and encounters that defy explanation. She began to research UFOs in 1985 and has since worked with hundreds of experiencers. Deborah was a great source of comfort for Stan with her innate ability to listen and provide reassurance.

A hypnotic regression seemed to be the best chance of getting some much needed answers. *Is he crazy?* I would wonder. *Am I crazy, for even entertaining the thought that this may not have been a dream? Maybe we are both nuts, and enabling each other's delusions.* I didn't believe that we were, but at this point I wasn't sure that the past few months' experiences hadn't made us both raving lunatics. We needed to get some answers to prove to ourselves that we were as sane as anyone else.

As the regression began, Deborah asked Stan, "Where do you find yourself now, when you say you're somewhere else?"

"I don't know where I am, it's really bright," Stan answered.

As I listened to the dialogue between Deborah and Stan, I began to comprehend that Stan was no longer in his apartment. For the first time I began to realize that what Stan was describing was real. This was not a dream. The feeling of awe cuffed me in the head, waking me up to the understanding that Stan could not be in his bedroom dreaming. He was reliving the sights and the smells that he was experiencing as he scanned the dimly lit room, eyes still tightly shut. I was consumed by the emotions I could see on his face and could almost feel his discomfort. As I watched him struggle to comprehend that he had been abducted, I sat transfixed, watching him relive his abduction experience. I knew there is no way he could be making this up.

Like a reader of a good book, Deborah looked as if she couldn't wait to find what hidden details she could uncover next. "What makes you think you're stuck to a wall?"

"I can't move my arms or legs. I can't move my body. It's like I'm sucked…or glued…to the wall. And I'm pissed," Stan replied.

Shock swept though me. *What in the hell is happening to this man I love?* I thought as I struggled to comprehend what Stan was trying to convey. I shifted to the edge of my seat in fear as I watched Stan's body contorting, struggling to free himself from an unseen force.

"What is keeping you connected to the wall, Stan?" Deb asked. With bated breath I waited for the answer.

"I don't know. I keep looking but I can't figure it out," Stan answered. "There's something around my wrists...I'm trying to get free...the three alien things are here...I can't get free...they're turning me around, and they're doing something to me... if I could move, I could hit one of 'em...I hear this thought in my head... the female alien is telling me somehow that it's okay, it's okay, it's okay...they're sticking a needle in my back...it's like a little suction thingy with a sharp, metal silver thing at the end...I can't describe it...I've never seen one before...the needle's attached to the tube... it's making a funny whirring noise...they're sticking it really far into my back...they're putting it in a...little box, and they close it... like a drawer kind of thing."[4]

Oh, my gawd, this really happened, I thought. It was not a dream. There was no doubt left in my mind—this was a real abduction. As I wiped the tears from my face, I wondered, *how is anything they're doing to Stan okay?* I now understood why Stan was fighting so hard to forget this experience, and was calling it a dream. It was a nightmare that he would never be able to wake up from or forget. It was real.

Watching this regression was as painful as holding my children while they got their baby shots. I knew he had to endure this so he could learn to deal with what he had experienced. Just like a baby needs immunizations to keep it safe, Stan needed to know he was not crazy so he could be healthy again. I was overwhelmed with sadness. This kind, sweet man that means the world to me had just relived possibly the most frightening ordeal of his life. I didn't know how to make it go away or how to protect him. What would my role in his life be now? I was at a loss.

---

[4] Romanek, *Messages*, 57-58

A few days later I called my friend Jill (pseudonym). "Hey Jill, can you come over please? I really need someone to talk to."

"Sure. What's wrong, Lisa? Are you okay?"

"Yes," I said. I just really need a friend right now. I will tell you about it when you get here."

I had told Jill about Stan's many UFO sightings and his "dream" weeks before. She was skeptical, and giggled a lot, but she was one of my best friends, and was at least willing to listen. This time around, I had to tell her I thought what he was referring to as a dream was really a true abduction. Jill arrived about five minutes later. She knew by the look on my face that something had really upset me.

"What's wrong? Are the kids okay?"

I started to tell her the story of the regression, and what Stan had remembered after feeling the tap on the back of his head while on the deck with the three aliens in his supposed dream. She sat and held my hand as I told her the entire story. She didn't laugh this time. She could see that I was scared silly.

As I began to cry, I asked Jill, "What do I do? I know in my heart this is real. I can't just go to Colorado and make sure he doesn't get taken again. How do I keep him safe?"

Jill simply answered, "You can't do anything right now. You are too upset to drive anyway. I'm here for you, I'm sorry if I did not believe you before when you told me about the UFOs and the alien dream. Hell, I still don't know if I believe it, but you do. So, as your friend I will help you get through this."

"Jill, thanks for being here, you're the only person I can talk to about this. I tried to talk to Kim, but she decided that Stan was just crazy, and that I needed to stay as far away from him as possible."

"Kim is such a bitch," Jill teased. "I say we go string all her underwear together and run them up her TV antenna. That will teach her for laughing at you, and for being mean to Stan."

Jill could always make me smile. She is one of the silliest people I have ever met.

I then reminded her that she laughed at me, too. "Well, then let's run all of Kim's bras up the antenna too, just because I was such a bitch for laughing at you. That will teach me a lesson, too."

I began to laugh, and Jill hugged me. "All better now?" she asked.

"Yes, I said. Thank God you live next door. Thanks for coming to let me cry on your shoulder. I'm okay now."

I realized then that laughter really was the best medicine. Stan is a strong man. I knew if I kept him laughing at his experiences, he would be alright. Realization hit me then and there, having a friend that supports you is critical.

Many people and websites online who discuss abduction tell you to keep your abductions a secret. I disagree wholeheartedly. If your friends don't support you, then they aren't good friends: find new ones. A good support system is important. I feel that it is imperative for our mental, spiritual, and even physical health to not hold it in. Talking about the fear relieves a lot of stress. If your listeners truly are your friends, they will learn to cope—family included. Jill didn't have to believe in the existence of aliens, or UFOs for that matter. She just needed to be my friend. I only had a handful of friends left after the custody suit, and Jill was the only one who supported me no matter what.

Many families who have experienced alien contact also deal with the rejection from friends, ridicule from fellow church goers, and being shunned by family members. I guess that is a natural response. The concept of aliens and UFOs is so far outside their realm of everyday thinking that it brings up too many fears.

While helping Stan through his experiences, I began to notice that there was a pattern of emotional responses to these sightings and abduction events; much the same as the emotional struggles experienced by the family members of the elderly population I cared for. I have come to realize that the abductees/experiencers and their families and friends go through a coping process much like dealing with a terminal diseases such as Alzheimer's disease, cancer, and even death. Abduction experiences also affect you in stages in much the same way. These feelings are to be expected, and they're normal.

Denial is the first step. Some experiencers of ET contact tend to withdraw from the world around them. Others may feel as though they must be having a bad dream and that they'll soon awaken from it. Most don't want to believe that aliens are real or that what they have experienced is possible.

The second step is anger. Experiencers and people close to them are angry that these experiences are happening to them. They may lash out at the people closest to them and not know why they are doing it. Anger may also lead to feelings of guilt.

Bargaining is the third step in this process. Many experiencers begin to bargain with themselves and others. If this will stop, I will be a better person. They imagine that if they promise to do this or that, God will return things to the way they used to be.

Like in the death process, the stage to follow is depression. For many, this can be the most difficult stage to get through. Signs of depression include a feeling of melancholy, unconcern about the outside world, or a loss of interest in eating and sleeping. Feelings of guilt, helplessness, hopelessness, and worthlessness are common.

The final stage is acceptance. As abductees deal with these experiences and accept that they are real, they come to understand and accept that they are beginning a new chapter in life. A new "normal" emerges, and in such a new understanding the happiness and laughter returns.

One afternoon I gave Stan an ultimatum: either he married me, or he went away. He didn't want to marry me for fear of bringing the UFO stuff into our lives. It was already very much a part of our lives. I couldn't live the nearly 400 miles apart any longer. Stan weaves this dramatic story of how I forced him to marry me using tears, threats, and bribery. I simply smile and agree. But that is exactly how it *didn't* happen.

4

Things That Go Bump in the Night

Stan and I married on July 27, 2002, in a beautiful ceremony in a quaint stone chapel nestled in the Rocky Mountains. I was a nervous wreck. Mark, Stan's sister, and a handful of my family were the only people that I knew of the nearly one hundred guests who had been invited. If any aliens were in attendance, I either didn't see them, or I assumed they were guests of Stan's.

A short, slightly plump woman, appearing to be in her late forties with an infectious smile, introduced herself to me. She and her husband were the first guests to arrive at the church.

"Hi, I'm Heather, and this is my husband, Gar," she said. "We are friends of Tiger's."

Tiger is Stan's middle name, and what most of his friends and family call him. Heather's magnetic personality and kindness instantly put me at ease. I knew she was destined to become one of my closer friends.

We went camping for our honeymoon, Stan, the kids, and I. Yes, the kids came with us. Sounds romantic, doesn't it? Our honeymoon destination: Rifle Falls, in Western Colorado. We had a great time hiking, playing in the falls, exploring the caverns, having picnic lunches, and grilling suppers. No flushing toilets, no shower houses, no stores close by, and no laundry rooms. Sounds like fun, right? It was an adventure to see who could stand being filthy the longest. *If Stan doesn't run from the sight of me in these three days of roughing it, he never will. He will never think badly of me in the morning.*

"Don't move," Stan whispered, shaking me awake our first night in the Rocky Mountains.

"What's wrong?" I whispered back, a little terrified.

"There is something outside the tent," he replied.

Oh, my gawd, the three aliens who had abducted Stan are outside the tent, I thought.

"What is it?" I whispered.

"If I tell you, you have to promise me that you won't move," he said in a hushed tone.

"I promise I won't move, just tell me what's going on," I whispered again.

"It's a bear. It came across the stream," Stan breathed.

Even though I promised that I would not move, a mixture of fear and excitement ran through me. I love bears, and wanted to see it. I took a deep breath to calm my racing heart. I remembered the kids' tent was angled four feet in front of our tent. Silently, I scooted out from under the covers, inching my way to the side of the tent. I was trying to peek out of the tent flap, making sure the bear wasn't going to wake up the kids while Stan fumbled through his rucksack to find his knife. We could hear the bear grunting and moving around, but the kids' tent was blocking it from my view. I could barely keep my excitement under control. Stan knew how much I loved these animals, and how hard it was for me not to rush out to glimpse the furry fellow. I was oblivious to the fact that I could be its midnight snack. Stan watched me like a hawk, making sure I stayed as quiet as possible.

"*Shhhh,*" Stan warned. "If the bear hears you he will come to investigate, and I will have to try and protect you and the kids. I don't want to get mauled, and I don't want to hurt the bear either."

"I know," I whispered. "I'm being quiet, but I want to see him, too."

We spent the next twenty minutes in near silence listening to the bear move around while trying to keep track of where it roamed. It was all very frustrating. Finally, all was silent. The bear had moved on, probably to the area where the dumpsters were located. I was so excited that I couldn't go back to sleep and neither could Stan.

The next morning, I couldn't wait to get out of the tent to look for signs of the bear's visit. The dirt all around the picnic table and on the picnic table was covered with its massive paw prints. They were as big as my son's head. Thank the Lord the kids stayed asleep. Needless to say that morning we moved to another campsite, away from the stream.

We enjoyed the nights sitting in our lawn chairs looking at the stars, trying to find the few constellations we knew. Life seemed calm again. Happiness enveloped us.

Upon our return to Denver, we loaded Stan's belongings and headed home to Nebraska. It was very hard for Stan to leave Colorado, but he agreed that it was a good idea. He had received this email in February 2002, five months before we were married.

Stan - for what it's worth, I received this tonight.
Jack

----- Original Message -----
From: "The Truth" <the_truth20500@lycos.com>
To: <jlandman@jman5.com>
Sent: Thursday, February 07, 2002 6:49 PM
Subject: About Mr. Romanek

Mr. Landman

Please take this seriously! I cannot tell you who I am
because I work for a government agency not many people
know about. I am risking my safety even emailing this
to you. I am doing so because you are a safe contact,
and everyone else involved is being watched to closely.
It is too risky for me to contact this person any other
way!

Not to long ago we were monitoring one of your shows
only because of the person you had as a guest that
evening. Unfortunately for Mr. Stan Romanek what has
been happening to him is not a coincidence. Something
big is going to happen in the next few years and
Mr. Romanek will be the key. This is the real deal!
Everything is about to be revealed. The problem is the
powers to be do not want this to happen because their
power structure might crumble. So you see Mr. Romanek's
safety is now in question and people disappear all
the time. Please get this to Mr. Romanek and let him
know the best thing he can do is get what he is going
through, out to the public. It will be safer for him!
Please understand Mr. Landman you have no idea how big
this is.

Stan needed to get out of the reach of the nuts that were calling him with death threats. They—who ever these people were—had a favorite fear tactic, telling Stan that the authorities would find his dismembered body in the desert if he didn't shut up and stop talking about what he had been seeing and experiencing. These threats became very serious to me. I received this email a month before the wedding. What I find interesting is that both emails were sent by the same person but with different email addresses.

----- Original Message -----
From: THE TRUTH the_truth20500@excite.com
To: [email address redacted]
Sent: Wednesday, June 19, 2002 4:52 PM
Subject: The Truth

This is regarding Stan Romanek. I understand this might be a little hard for you to except but it's all real. As you know by now this UFO case is very important. But what you don't know is how important! It seems that the people upstairs are making a statement and Mr. Romanek is the conduit. I for one would like to see this happen. But there are those in the organization I work for that do not. In fact the reason for this contact is so you know that Stan is in danger! I have tried to contact Mr. Romanek. But Stan is stubborn, and I am sure he believes these warnings to be a hoax. Unfortunately time is running out. It has taken a lot of work, but I have managed to keep your location out of the picture. So you are a safe haven for Stan. If at all possible I may need your help in convincing Stan in coming out there sooner than planned. I have contacted others in MUFON that have been working closely with Stan. I hope you don't take this lightly; there is a lot at stake here! You don't know how special Stan is! He is more then he appears, even to him self

Signed
Concerned Informer

Gio, the MUFON investigator, had also gotten an email from this individual, with basically the same warning. So, I felt that I had to take it seriously. I wasn't taking any chances with Stan's life, it was imperative that Stan get as far away from Denver as possible. I naively thought that I could hide him from the threats, the aliens, and the UFO's in the middle of nowhere—small town Nebraska.

"Do you think we will ever move back to Colorado?" Stan asked.

"Sure, when the kids are older. Right now, I can't afford to make my ex mad again. I don't want to go through another court room battle," I told him.

We agreed that someday we would move back. I knew my ex-husband wouldn't allow me to move the kids anytime in the near future. Our new life was beginning. Our adventures as a family were just starting, and I wanted to enjoy them to the fullest.

One night a month or so after returning from our honeymoon, I woke up to hear Stan talking to someone.

"They are coming," he said.

When I sat up in bed I saw Stan walking around the dark room. With three windows in our bedroom he took turns going to each window repeating the same phrase.

"They're coming. I feel it. They're coming."

Then he came back to bed and was sound asleep within seconds. He never said another word. He just went back to sleep. I didn't know who Stan was talking to, but I thought, *Whoooo hoooo, I think I married a nutball.*

Humor got me through the incident of his night-babbling. I just laid there watching Stan sleep, giggling and thinking about the first time this babbling had occurred. It was on one of the trips I had made to visit Stan in Colorado. We were staying in a remote cabin resort. During the night, Stan had gotten out of bed and was standing by the window talking to himself.

"I need to go get some chicken," he said. I started to laugh out loud at his insistence. I tried to talk to him but he did not respond.

"I need to go now. I have to go get chicken." As my laughter continued it became apparent that, for some reason, Stan had to go get chicken, and he was going to do just that, naked as a jay bird.

As he headed for the door, I jumped out of bed, and caught him by the arm.

"Stan, you can't get chicken. It's one o'clock in the morning, and all of the restaurants are closed." His reaction was so strong it was as if I had slapped him. He jumped back from me with a look on his face of fear mixed with confusion.

"What?" he retorted. "Why do you want me to go get chicken? Are you crazy?"

His statement made me laugh hard. "No Stan, I'm not crazy, but I am wondering about you right now," I replied. I got Stan back into bed, and as we lay there talking, he started shaking.

He whispered, "I'm afraid that something or someone was trying to draw me outside."

"I will protect you, you are safe with me, but you are not going outside naked. And definitely not to go get chicken," I giggled. "Besides, restaurants require not only shoes and shirts for service, they also require pants." We both laughed for a little while, and eventually fell back to sleep.

I am amazed that, even with the sleepless nights and the fear of abduction, the stress of keeping this all a secret from my family, friends, and kids was not making me angry at Stan. I married this man for better or for worse, for richer or for poorer. So far it was better and poorer, but I loved him. I was determined not to let the stress of these weird experiences get in the way of our happiness.

A few nights later (August 30, 2002) we awoke to a horrible lightning storm. Lightning was flashing every few seconds. It was incredible. Stan was scared that the aliens had found him again. I, being the smart aleck that I am, simply stated, "Well, at least they are not afraid to park in the front yard." I thought it was funny.

Stan, on the other hand, didn't find any humor in my statement. He was out of bed like a shot, searching out of the windows for something sinister lurking in the bushes. He was also afraid the lightning storm would turn into a tornado.

"Honey, it's just a lightning storm. Don't worry about it. And come back to bed."

"Come on, Lisa. Please get up and come with me. Let's go see what is going on outside," he begged.

"*Ummm,* no," I said. "I have to go to work in the morning. Why don't you get out the video camera and tape the storm. I will watch it tomorrow."

The next afternoon, I watched the video he shot the night before. Stan and I were shocked to see a red orb on the ground in front of my van. It was spinning, traveling into the front yard, and back into the street. Neither of us had ever seen anything like it before. We had more evidence now, not that we knew what to do with it other than document it. Things seemed to be getting scary now in Nebraska. My mind was racing. *Why is this happening? I thought getting him out of Colorado would make it all stop!*

A few days later, I awoke thinking it was time to get up for work. I looked at the alarm clock that was on my dresser across the room. Something was wrong with it. I could not figure out what time it was—it really made no sense. I woke Stan up and asked him if he could tell me what time it was. He looked over at the clock and was as confused as I was. I laid there for about five minutes thinking about how tired I was, but I couldn't go back to sleep. I got up and went over to turn off the alarm, and found the reason for my confusion. Somehow, my alarm clock was upside down on my dresser. It was about 6:00 a.m., so I decided I might as well get up and get ready for work. Making myself some coffee, I went out to the back yard to enjoy a cup.

Stan came outside a few minutes later with papers in his shaking hands. He handed them to me.

"What the hell is going on?" he yelled. The fear could be heard in his voice. "Did they take me again?"

"What is this?" I took the pages of paper he handed to me, having no idea what I was looking at. They looked like mathematical equations of some sort.

"There are pencils and ink pens all over the floor, and in the bed. Why are they in the bed?" Stan asked.

I tried to pay attention to what he was saying while concentrating on the pages that made no sense. Stan continued to become more and more agitated that I would not respond to his question.

First sleeping equation. Photo by Stan Romanek.

"Why would you do this?" Stan yelled. "I don't understand. Are you trying to make me think I am crazy?"

That got my attention—my full attention. He was ticking me off. Stan has an innate ability to say the wrong things when he is freaked out, and they have a way of ticking me off to no end.

"What? Are you kidding me, you think I did this? Maybe you *are* crazy!" I snapped. "You must be, if you think I would waste my time throwing pens and pencils all over the room, and in our bed. I don't know what any of this means but it sure as hell has nothing to do with me. I had noticed the pens on the floor by the desk, but I thought the cats had dumped the pencils on the floor. I didn't know they were also in our bed."

"I'm sorry. I know you didn't do it. I'm just really freaked out right now."

"Maybe you should go call Gio and let him know what is going on," I suggested. "Maybe he or Deborah can explain what may have happened, because I sure don't know."

Later that day, I called the MUFON investigator Gio, "What do you think these math equations mean?"

"I don't know, these new equations don't mean Stan was abducted again," Gio explained. "Abductees/experiencers can have a lot of information from previous abductions stored in their minds. This information can come out when they least expect it, and not always when it is convenient or comfortable for the person. It's like a filing cabinet drawer. Think of it as if some of the files are in sideways, and the drawer is jammed shut, and doesn't open all the way. Sometimes you can get the drawer open enough to peek inside. And sometimes you can force the drawer open, and stuff flies all over."

"What happens if we force the drawer open?" I asked.

"I don't know for sure what would happen, but it could be devastating to Stan. That drawer I metaphorically refer to contains a lot of repressed memories that Stan has tucked away for safe keeping. Perhaps some of the information that is stored there was put there by the ETs to come out at certain times, when it is appropriate for him to remember," Gio explained. "If it's forced open and he has to remember too much too soon, he may not be able to deal with it."

"I, for one, don't want to find out at the expense of Stan's mental health," I said. "He already feels like he's losing his mind."

Gio and I agreed that for Stan's sake and sanity we did not want to force him to remember too much too soon. Stan was not yet ready to know what else had happened to him. He was not completely able to deal with what had already been revealed in his previous regression with Deborah.

A year or so after Stan had written this equation, Gio had found a physicist at the University of Nebraska. Jack Kasher, Ph.D., took on the daunting task of figuring out what the equation meant, if anything. I don't expect this material to be easily absorbed. It's still way over my head. But providing any and all analyses of these experiences is what's important. Here is Dr. Kasher's report:

Interpretation of Stan Romanek's Symbols, Equations, and Drawings
by Jack Kasher, Ph.D.
Page, Written 09/03/2002 during the night

The second and third lines of this page are explanations and approximations of the terms used in the first line, so let's start with them.

$\alpha = e^2 / \hbar c \sim 1/137$

This is the fine structure constant used in quantum electrodynamics. The funny symbol used here by Stan has to be the Greek letter alpha, since $e^2 / \hbar c$ is the fine structure constant, and alpha is the symbol used for it. c has been defined above. $\hbar$ is Plank's constant h divided by 2π, where h is 6.62×10^{-27} erg-seconds. e is the charge on the electron, which is 4.8×10^{-10} in esu units (1.6×10^{-19} coulombs in mks units).

$\lambda e \equiv \hbar / mc \sim 10^{-11}$ cm

This is the Compton wavelength of the electron. m is the mass of the electron. Determining the position of an electron to within this distance requires enough energy to create another electron. The exact value of the Compton wavelength of the electron is 3.86×10^{-11} cm.

The mc written next appears in the first line, with m again being the mass of the electron, and c the speed of light in vacuum. Possibly trying to explain this term, Stan follows this with

$mc^2 \sim \frac{1}{2}$ MeV

This is the rest mass of the electron given in millions of electron volts. The exact value is 0.511 MeV. Notice that Stan uses the precise notation of capital M, small e, and capital V.

$L^2_p \sim 10^{-66}$ cm^2

This is the square of the Planck length, and is sometimes referred to as the Planck area. Physicists suspect that quantum gravity will become important for understanding physics at about this scale. Taking the square root, $L_p \sim 10^{-33}$ cm. The exact value is calculated from $L_p = (\hbar G / c^3)^{1/2} = 1.61 \times 10^{-33}$ cm, where G is the gravitational constant, 6.67×10^{-8} dyne-cm^2/gram^2. It is curious that Stan writes L_p as the square of the Planck length, rather than just the length itself. This requires him to square the 10^{-33} to get 10^{-66}.

Now, to the top line on this page.

$-8\pi e^2/\lambda e^2 L_p{}^2$

This is the third term in the top line. The fourth term, -10^{73} GeV/cm^3, shows that the units for each of the five terms is energy per unit volume. If in the third term we insert the value for e, 4.8×10^{-10} esu, and the approximations for L_p and λ_e, 10^{-33} cm and 10^{-11} cm, and convert to GeV/cm^3 (1.6×10^{-3} erg $= 1$ GeV), we get -3.62×10^{73} GeV/cm^3, which corresponds to his $\sim -10^{73}$ GeV/cm^3. If, on the other hand, we insert the exact values for L_p and λ_e, namely 1.61×10^{-33} cm and 3.86×10^{-11} cm, we get 9.37×10^{71} GeV/cm^3 $\sim 10^{72}$ GeV/cm^3, which does not quite match the 10^{73}. So Stan (or whoever) is using the approximations for L_p and λ_e when making the calculations. This makes it even more unlikely that Stan could find these expressions in any textbook.

This term can be written $8\pi(-e^2/\lambda_e)/\lambda_e L_p{}^2$. The expression in parentheses is the electrostatic or binding energy between an electron and a positron which are a distance λ_e apart. As we will see next, when we look at the second term, this is also equal to αmc^2, the fine structure constant times the rest energy of the electron. So these terms are not just random letters thrown together, but have some physical meaning.

$-8\pi\alpha mc/\lambda_e L_p{}^2$

This is the second term in the top line. If we equate the second and third terms, as Stan does, after canceling the 8, π, $L_p{}^2$, and one of the λ_e, we are left with $\alpha mc = e^2/\lambda_e$. Substituting $\lambda_e \equiv \hbar/mc$, we have amc = $e^2mc/\hbar$, or a = $e^2/\hbar$ = $(e^2/\hbar c)c$ = αc. So in the second term a = αc, the fine structure constant time the speed of light. Thus the second term is

$$-8\pi\alpha mc^2 / \lambda_e L_p^2.$$

When numbers are substituted into this expression, we get -9.37×10^{72} GeV/cm^3 ~ -10^{73} GeV/cm^3, which matches Stan's approximation given in the fourth term. The reason for the difference in the two calculations is that in going from the third term to the second term I used the exact value of λ_e instead of Stan's approximation.

So the second, third, and fourth terms in the top line match; and, in addition, we have found out that the a in the second term must be the fine structure constant times the speed of light, a = αc.

A final note about this term, $-8\pi\alpha mc^2 / \lambda_e L_p^2$. Something close to this, $-L_p^{-3}\alpha m_e c^2$ = $-\alpha m_e c^2 / L_p^3$, appears in footnote 13 of Jack Sarfatti's article *The Micro-Quantum Vacuum, 4th draft, 11/14/2002* (I've underlined the relevant line).

[13] We do not need the electron-phonon interaction here as in a real superconductor with real electron-electron pairs. The Fermi momentum is ~ h/L_p. The binding energy is the virtual pair is ~ $\alpha m_p c^2$ ~ -10^{17} Gev ~ critical temperature to destroy vacuum superconductivity. <u>The condensation energy density is ~ $-L_p^{-3}(m_e /$ $m_p)\alpha m_e c^2$ ~ $-L_p^{-3}\alpha m_e c^2$ ~ 10^{99} 10^{-2} Mev/cc.</u> The photon rest mass is ~ 10^{-65} gm with a Meissner penetration depth ~ 10^{28} cm, so that the ratio of penetration depth to coherence length of the macro-quantum vacuum >> 1, i.e. a hard superconductors (sic) with magnetic vortex string topological defects.

If we drop the 8π, what is left of the second term, $-\alpha mc^2 / \lambda_e L_p^2$, is very close in form to this condensation energy density, $-\alpha m_e c^2 / L_p^3$. the difference is that λ_e has been substituted for one of the L_p, so that we have $\lambda_e L_p^2$ instead of L_p^3. I don't know what the physical interpretation of Stan's term would be.

$10^{-45} \, m_p c^2 / L_p^3$

This is the last term in the top line. This term apparently was included because the "writer" wants to show us that the energy density in the second, third, and fourth terms is not beyond what is physically possible. The last term includes the Planck mass, m_p. This is the mass whose Compton wavelength, $\hbar/mc$, is equal to its Schwartzschild radius, $2Gm/c^2$. This latter is the radius a mass would have if it becomes a black hole. When the Compton wavelength is equated to the Schwatzschild radius the 2 is not included in the latter, so that the two lengths will be equal to the Planck length, instead of 2.28×10^{-33} cm. Equating $\hbar/mc$ to Gm/c^2 and solving for the mass leads to $m_p = 2.177 \times 10^{-5}$ grams. The largest energy density possible is the expression given in the last term in line 1, $m_p c^2 / L_p^3$. Inserting the exact values for m_p and c and the approximation 10^{-33} cm for L_p into the last term, $10^{-45} \, m_p c^2 / L_p^3$, and converting to GeV/cm³, we are left with $10^{-45} \times 1.22 \times 10^{118}$ GeV/cm³ $= 1.22 \times 10^{73}$ GeV/cm³ $\sim 10^{73}$ GeV/cm³, as needed.

$d\Delta w_x / dV$

This is the first term in the top line. It appears that the V is volume, since all the rest of the terms have volume in the denominator. I am not certain that the w_x is correct. It cannot be $\omega_x = 2\pi f_x$, the angular frequency in the x direction, since the units of ω are 1/time, and the term in the numerator must have units of energy. So I am not certain what this term is. The Δ indicates that it is a small amount of whatever w_x is. The d in both numerator and denominator indicates that this term is the rate of change of Δw_x with respect to volume; i.e., the derivative of Δw_x with respect to volume.

I should point out here that the term in the denominator appears to actually be ∂V, and not dV. Perhaps Stan just didn't finish the downward stroke on the d. In any case, ∂V is incorrect. You could also ask him for the physical significance of the energy densities expressed in the second and third terms, and why he chose to use $\lambda_e L_p^2$ for the volume.

If Stan is hypnotized again, it would be good to ask him what he means by this first term—what is the "w_x" and what is meant by the Δw_x and its rate of change with volume.

This completes the analysis of the top line. Now let's look at the rest of the page.

$V = n \times a \times dB/dT$

I interpret these symbols to be what I have written here. If I am correct, the two x's appear to indicate that the n, a, and dB/dT should be multiplied together. If the funny symbol between the x's is an a, then this equation is a specific case of Faraday's Law, which shows the magnitude of the voltage V generated by a magnetic induction changing with time, dB/dT, inside a constant area a. The n would be the number of coils in the wire surrounding the constant area. There would normally be a minus sign before the n on the right side, and the use of a instead of A would be unusual, but not incorrect. The use of a might be a stretch, since Stan quite clearly writes a nice A in the expression immediately below this.

But he also wrote a strange symbol for the fine structure constant, instead of the α.

If this expression is Faraday's Law, I'm not sure how it fits in with the rest of the page. If it is not Faraday's Law, then I don't know what it is. If V is a volume, as in the first line, then it probably is one that is shrinking, because of the last line on the page. The two x's cannot indicate a double vector cross product, since V on the left side is a scalar, whether it is volume or voltage, and n should not be a vector.

The first symbol on the last line could be interpreted as positronium, which is an electron (negative charge) and positron (positive charge) bound together and circling one another. The next symbol seems to indicate that they circle closer and closer, spiraling in toward one another, until they get close enough to become a black hole. This is stretching things a little bit; but I am trying to make sense out of the symbols and equal signs. The next term,

$$A \rightarrow 4\pi(2GM/c^2)^2$$

indicates to me that a spherical surface area is shrinking to the size of the surface area of a black hole, which is what the $4\pi(2GM/c^2)^2$ is. This might lead to a gravitational field dense enough for the creation of a wormhole, shown by the two curved lines with the curly one in between, like the ones on Stan's other page.

At the bottom of the page the straight line with dots at each end, followed by the curved line, also with dots at the ends, are the same as on the first page. Again, these may indicate that flat space can be curved, so that one can travel quickly from one point to the other (i.e., from one dot to the other) through a wormhole.

***

I was trying to be supportive of Stan and his experiences, but I was getting sick of the weirdness in our lives. The ET stuff was supposed to go away. I wanted it to stop, and for us to be able to live normal lives. Everyday life was getting increasingly confusing. The sleepless nights were becoming more frequent, and when we finally did get to sleep, we were waking up repeatedly during the night. Stress and fear-induced insomnia. It was not that I didn't want to sleep, I was exhausted. Beyond exhausted. But the fear of what might happen during the night prevented me from getting the rest that I needed.

Stan would move in bed, and I would wake up thinking he was being taken or that he would once again start writing equations in the night. Many nights, we would simply lie in bed talking. On one such night, when sleep eluded us, I shared with Stan my thoughts about the aliens. I had very little prior knowledge of these space invaders beyond what Stan had shared after his abduction. However, being exposed to this aspect of reality at this point in my life has led me to think about things more unconventionally; to think like I never have before in my life. With these truths staring me in the face, I began to question what I suddenly knew but had not researched.

"You know what, Stan? I feel that the aliens are curious about our emotions. I wonder if they are drawn to us because of them, or if in some cases they incite them. I wonder if it is just another part of their monitoring, learning how we deal with certain emotions, learning what responses happen in certain situations."

"It's a possibility, but I don't think they have emotions, at least not like we do," Stan replied.

"Imagine not having any emotions," I said. "No sadness, no happiness, no fear, no love, no joy, no hate, no feeling of surprise, shock. No pleasure in the smell of a rose, or the taste of a BBQ steak; the feeling of contentment when a babies cheek is next to yours, no knowledge of the emotion connected to seeing a sunset. No understanding of the love between a mother and child, or a husband and wife. Can you imagine?" I pondered aloud. "I can imagine, however, if the negative feelings went away. What a wonderful world we would live in if we had no war, no hate, no sadness, no loneliness, no prejudice. Never having to feel those emotions would be amazing."

As I pondered these thoughts, as I often did, I came to the conclusion that these emotions are what separate the men from the boys; or the humans from the aliens. The ETs don't seem to depend on these emotions to function like we do. I think that is one of the reasons they are so fascinated with us. We are fountains of emotions every second of every day, and we display them in so many ways.

Years later in doing research to learn more about the aliens and their emotions, I came across David Jacob's website: International Center for Abduction Research (ICAR). David M. Jacobs, Ph.D., is an American historian and associate professor of History at Temple University, specializing in twentieth century American history and culture. Dr. Jacobs wrote an article titled *"Telepathy and Emotion in Alien Society,"* in which he states:

> *"Abductees report that alien emotional range seems to be greatly circumscribed. It is possible that telepathy restricts the range of emotions that can be transmitted and/or received. They seem to display satisfaction, excitement, a limited form of happiness, and even a limited form of fondness. Conversely, they can become frustrated, annoyed, surprised, peeved, and even irritated. Abductees sometimes describe aliens having*

an extremely rudimentary sense of humor, especially when dealing with human children."[7]

In general, abductees don't report seeing aliens crying, becoming enraged, expressing sincere love or unrestrained joy, fighting with each other, or having their feelings hurt.

Human beings experience contrasting emotions, love and hate being the most prevalent. However, even when we are furious with the people we care about, we still love them. We fight, we make up. We cry, we laugh.

I now understood how unique the human experience is, how precious it is. We humans are exceptional, amazing, spiritual, emotional creatures. We have passion. Passion makes us different from all other living creatures on earth, and perhaps beyond. It seems even "advanced beings" struggle to understand how we perceive and express ourselves.

I love my husband, abductee or not, and was committed to making my marriage work, in spite of the circumstances that were invading and controlling our lives. I would not allow the stress of these bizarre events to cause division between Stan and me. We would work through all of these events together, and learn how to process each event as it presented itself. Humor and laughter does a lot to relieve stress-filled minds. And over time I came to realize humor to be the best antidote.

It was time to liven up our lives and stop concentrating on all of the scary negative influences. It was time to plan another

---

[5] David M. Jacobs, "Part 11: Emotions, Telepathy, and the Visual Arts," *Telepathy and Emotion in Alien Society*, 2004, www.ufoabduction.com/telepathy11.htm

camping trip, and have some fun. Little did I know it was about to be the most mind-boggling camping trip of our lives.

5

Camping Follies

Extraterrestrial contact and alien abduction can terrify all concerned, upending their lives, bringing chaos into family dynamics. To me, learning how to face such situations allowed me to take my personal power back. Homesickness had hit Stan like a Nebraska tornado. He longed for his friends in Colorado. So, we called Mark and invited him to come to Nebraska and go camping with us.

Mark drove 370 miles from Denver, Colorado, having bought a new tent, sleeping bag, and other camping gear he would need. Exhaustion wore on him like his sweaty t-shirt. When he arrived we decided to let him rest, even though we had already stuffed our camping gear, food, and supplies into the van. However, we couldn't stop ourselves from first showing Mark the orb video Stan had recently caught in front yard during the storm, as well as disclose the uncanny night writing.

Mark was fascinated by the video, and totally dumfounded by the equations. "What is this, Tiger?"

"Hell if I know. I woke up one morning with a pen sticking me in the leg, and this paper wedged in my armpit. I don't know what it means, or where it came from. All I know is that it is my handwriting, but I have no recollection of writing it. My life is getting more and more bizarre by the day, and it scares the crap out of me."

"I have never seen anything like it before. Is it math of some kind?" Mark asked.

"I really don't know, but those chicken scratches are more proof that something very strange is going on."

"Does Lisa know how to write this stuff?"

"No, and don't ask her if she did it, I made that mistake already. She yelled at me. What do you think I should do with it?"

"Hang on to it, and put it somewhere safe. I don't know anyone who can tell you what it means, or even what it is."

"Okay, you guys, enough talk of aliens and equations. We're supposed to be getting ready to go camping. Hop to it, get your stuff loaded into the van so we can get on the road," I told them.

Stan, still trying to adjust to his new home, began complaining to Mark about the horrible storms. The weather conditions in Nebraska in early September are at times daunting, with 100 degree temperatures accompanied by ninety percent humidity. Thunderstorms can pop up out of nowhere, sometimes accompanied by tornadoes. Where we lived stood right in the middle of Tornado Alley. Weather like this could crop up at any time. Living in the overcrowded metropolis of Denver had obviously insulated them from wide open spaces. Without the mountain to point them west, they had no sense of direction, no security, and no protection from storms.

The sun beat down on a hot and humid day, with the katydids singing loudly; a beautiful day for camping. After driving the forty miles to Harlan County Lake, the arduous job of setting up camp commenced. Our tents were nestled under a canopy of massive cottonwood trees, eighty yards from the edge of the lake. The bathhouse sat 500 yards behind our campsite. Being within walking distance of the bathrooms was a necessity especially at night.

Stan and Mark made quick work of assembling the tents. The kids scrambled into their swimming suits and ran to play in the lake. I sat up the grill and began preparing supper. Grabbing their fishing poles, the guys meandered to the lake to relax in the water-cooled shade, trying their luck at fishing. I could hear squeals of laughter coming from the lake. Looking toward the lake, I witnessed Mark and Stan abandon their fishing poles and jump into the lake, joining the kids. Letting the kids jump off their shoulders into the water, they elicited more screams of joy. I set up the picnic table for supper, smiling as I listened to the fun they were all having. *Camping is exactly what we needed to forget about the UFOs and aliens,* I thought.

After calling everyone for supper, five soggy swimmers all ran into camp, surrounding me in an obvious pre-planned bear hug attack to get me as wet as they were. The next couple of hours were spent relaxing, visiting, and enjoying the warm evening lake air.

Night's shadows began creeping in, stretching its long tentacles into the peaceful beauty of our surroundings. The eerie ambience transforming the looming cottonwood trees branches into monstrous fingers of fear. The night suddenly became ominously oppressive. The rustling of the leaves and the lapping of the waves were putting us on alert. Every noise was suddenly suspect. The usual nighttime fear of aliens were creeping into my mind. *Will the aliens find us? Will we be safe sleeping outside under the stars?* Mark and the kids had scurried to the security of their tents, exhaustion claiming them for the night.

Needing to make one more trip to the restroom before surrendering to the safety of my makeshift bed, I nervously asked, "Stan will you walk with me to the bathroom?"

"Sure, I'll go with you. I want to go watch the bats anyway," Stan announced, deciding to have a little fun with me.

"Bats, what bats?" I shuddered in disgust.

"The ones by the bathroom," he smirked. "Let's go, I'll show you." My fear of the dark suddenly amplified. *I'll never get to sleep now,* I thought. My adolescent fear of vampires has infused my adult life with genuine anxiety. I suffer from chiroptophobia, a fear of bats.

"Oh *gawd.* Really? Bats? Can you scare them away?" I begged.

A light pole in front of the bathhouse shone like a dim beacon in the night, allowing us to find our way to and from the bathroom. It emanated a sense of security from the darkness that loomed over the campground. Bats plunged into the glow of the bug-filled light, swooping in and out of sight. I screamed, as I ran for the building. The doors to the bathroom faced the blackness of the woods. I quickly dashed around the corner and into the brightly lit room. Relief flooded me. I had escaped the night and survived the onslaught of bats. I could hear Stan laughing behind me as I ran. Before exiting the "bathouse," I peeked around both corners and into the darkness of the woods. Fear of unknowns lurked in the eerie shadows making my imagination run wild. Half expecting something to jump out and grab me, I ran the short distance to the front of the bath enclosure where Stan was supposed to be waiting for me. There was no way was I getting under that bat infested light pole. Stan ambled toward the trees west of the bathhouse. "Stan, where are you going?" I snapped, pressing my back against the side of the brick building. A mantra was sounding in my brain, *Don't look up, don't look up…just don't look up.*

"Lisa, come look at this. Do you see that?" Keeping low, so not to be detected by the winged rodents, I ran under the light like a hunchback to Stan's side. Stan was pointing at a light hovering in the western sky, visible just above the treetops. *First bats, now what?!*

"Yes, I see it. What is that?"

"I'm not sure. I think it's a UFO," he stammered. Fear swept through me like a cold wind, chilling me to the bone. Pressing my trembling body against Stan's side for safety, I peeked up into the sky at the object. Stan pushed away from me, and proceeded to take out his key chain with a multitude of different colored lights Mark had given him. The object we were scrutinizing seemed to change colors as Stan shone the different lights at it.

"Is it just me, or is that thing getting closer?" he asked.

Barely holding back tears, I answered, "I don't know Stan, can we go back to the campsite now? I'm really scared." The mental mantra returned, *Don't look up, just don't look up.*

"Holy shit, run, its coming after us!" Stan screamed. Dread swept though me. Stan tore past me like a jack rabbit. Terror stricken, I began running for my life. *Am I going to be sucked up into a beam of light?* I screamed in my head. Would I ever be seen again? *Oh, my gawd, he's leaving me alone.* I tried to yell his name, but I had no breath. Would I ever make it to the camp site?

Just at that moment Stan and I collided in the darkness. *He came back for me.* He grabbed my arm and started running again. I felt like a cartoon character, my legs whirling in the air, my feet barely touching the ground. As Stan bounded through the undergrowth, with me in tow, I just knew they were now going to take us both. Stan ran like the wind dragging me behind him like a kite. *Why didn't we just stay with the damn bats?* Just then, I could see the tents beckoning. "Hurry!" they seemed to say. "We'll save you!"

Like charging bulls, the two of us came crashing into the campsite, coming to an abrupt halt in front of Mark's tent. Gasping for air, Stan began violently shaking his tent.

"Wake up, Mark, there's a UFO! Mark, get up, we need help!" Convinced that the UFO would be hovering above us at any second, Stan's frantic pleas for help continued. "Wake up, Mark! It's an emergency."

"What's wrong? What's going on, Tiger?" Mark frantically asked. He scrambled out of his tent, holding his t-shirt down to cover his undies.

"Hurry, Mark, hurry. There's a UFO up there. Hurry, put some damn pants on," Stan hollered. Numbly I stood transfixed, searching the sky. Fear of abduction caused my entire body to shake violently from teeth to toes. Silent tears fell down my cheeks as I rubbed my now aching shoulder. I scanned my feet to assure myself that I hadn't lost my shoes.

"Oh my *gosh*, really?" Mark's delight hung in the air. I couldn't believe how *excited* he was. He stood there giddy as a girl. He reached into his tent and snatched a pair of pants, quickly wiggling into them. Stan's angst began to decrease with his best friend by his side. Like two little boys on a secret mission, they began scanning the night sky, searching for signs of alien craft and purveying the threat of invasion.

Mark jubilantly exclaimed, "Well, Tiger, let's go see this UFO. It obviously didn't follow you down here." Mark didn't exhibit any of the fear Stan and I were experiencing. Stan seized my hand again, dragging me along once more. This time, *toward* the UFO. Mark could barely contain his excitement as he loped towards the shower houses with us in close pursuit. Mark's utmost dream has been to see a UFO up close and, ultimately, be abducted. Maybe this would be his chance. Mark has been researching UFOs for years and has heard the horror stories that people share of their encounters. Why would anyone, in their right mind, that is, want to be taken? The trauma and life-long scars of alien encounters cause emotional, physical, and mental unrest and has ruined people's lives. Only a fool would offer himself up for abduction. It just made no sense to me.

As we neared the bat house once again, I shuddered as Mark put on a serious face. The UFO investigator in him was no longer smiling, but the twinkle in his eyes conveyed his inner emotion of pure delight. Stan then pointed out the craft, hovering once again, just above the treetops. Armed with only a flashlight, Mark crashed through the woods, darkness quickly swallowing him. Stan and I retreated from the trail not willing to venture toward the object. The minutes ticked by, and seemed more like hours as we waited for Mark's return. Hesitantly, we edged back to the trail, hoping Mark would re-emerge soon.

Becoming alarmed, I finally asked Stan, "Do you think they took Mark? He has been gone a long time." *So much for leaving the UFOs and aliens at home,* I thought. "Oh crap, how will we explain this to anyone? If Mark is abducted and they don't bring him back, what will we tell people?"

"Are you kidding me? They won't keep Mark. They'll kick his butt out for trying to fly the spaceship and messing with everything," Stan joked, trying to calm my fear.

A flash of light captured our attention. Mark came scrambling up the trail toward us. He kept glancing over his shoulder again and again, as if he were being chased. The seriousness of his expression put me on alert. *Get ready to run.*

"Oh, thank God you're alright," I called to him. As he approached he looked over his shoulder again, shaking his head and saying nothing.

"What is it Mark? Is it still out there? Did you see it?" Stan questioned.

"Yeah, I saw it. It's still out there. Do you want me to show you?" Mark asked.

"Hell no, I don't want you to show me." Stan shifted back and forth on the balls of his feet, still looking up the pathway nervously. "What's it doing? Did you see any aliens?"

Mark ignored his questions, continuing to ask his own. "Are you sure, Tiger? It's not far away, it's only a ways up the path," Mark chuckled.

"I don't want to see it. Are you kidding me? It's still up there. And you're laughing. I'm confused, Mark. Tell me what's so damn funny." Finally, bursting into peals of laughter, Mark explained, "You know where you saw the UFO? Well that's where the RV Park is located. I can almost guarantee the people in that RV are just as freaked out as you are. They are probably considering the possibility of ETs, too. And all because some idiot is out here shinning colored lights into their camper windows not knowing their television isn't a UFO."

"Holy crap," Stan squealed. "Are you serious? Let's get out the hell out of here before they call the Ranger."

As we hastily skittered back to our campsite, laughter erupted from within with a deep sense of relief.

"I'm glad I put my pants on," Mark snickered.

The folly, the fear, and the flight of the imagination taught me a lesson I'd never forget. Things aren't always as they seem! We each learned lessons that night. Mark learned to sleep lightly and with his pants on. I learned that running without Stan dragging me is preferable, but not mandatory. Stan learned that there is a huge difference between a TV and a UFO. But the most important thing we learned from this camping trip is to laugh at ourselves and our shortcomings. No matter how scary a situation may appear it may not be as bad as you think, unless there are bats involved.

6

Fear of the Dark

Homeland Security took on a whole new meaning at our house. Stan insisted that the ETs had found him, that the red orbs in the yard were monitoring us. He became obsessed with the need to move—to escape the aliens somehow. That was the plan: move as soon as possible.

We moved from Holdrege, Nebraska, a town of 3,500 people to Kearney, Nebraska, a city of 35,000, hoping that more people meant less chance of detection from the ETs. I realize how paranoid it sounds, but when you are in this situation you can talk yourself into almost anything that makes you feel safe, even for a little while. I was willing to do whatever it took to make Stan feel safe. It didn't occur to me at that time that when Stan's first abduction had occurred, he lived in Lakewood, a suburb of Denver. If one million people didn't prevent abduction, why did we think 35,000 people would? Was I delusional? No. Just scared.

The evening of November 17, 2002 began like most nights at our house. The kids had showered and were in bed at 9:30. Stan and I watched the news and headed for bed around 10:30. As we snuggled with each other, a contented sigh escaped my lips as I drifted off to sleep.

I jolted awake to a horrible banging at my bedroom window. My heart leapt from my chest in fright. Someone was yelling my name. The banging started again. Screams for help sounded. "Lisa, please wake up. Help me, please."

What in the world is going on? Why is Stan outside in the middle of the night? I peeked through the blinds. Stan's face pressed against the window. Terror shone from his eyes. With fear gripping at my stomach, I ran to the locked family-room doors, flinging them open while flipping on the porch light. There stood Stan wearing only his boxer shorts, the frigid Nebraska night air flooding in. Dried blood covered his nose and the lower half of his face.

"What the hell happened to you? What are you doing outside?" I shouted.

"I don't know. I woke up on the ground next to the garage under the apple tree." As I looked past Stan to the area described, a flattened circle of grass shimmered like silver under the moonlight. Stan staggered forward, clutching his rib area on the right side as I pulled him into the family room, slamming the door behind him. As I continued to pull him through the family room and into the kitchen, I looked at the wall clock—3:00 a.m. He was so cold that he had a pale-blue tint to his skin. He seemed unable to tell me what had happened and why he had been outside. I began rubbing his arms and back to warm him. He was shaking hard. The more I tried to calm the shaking the more I realized it was more than the cold affecting him. As I rubbed his back, my hand hit a saucer-sized patch of wounds. I said through my tears, "I am so sorry, Honey; it's happened again."

The reality of what had happened penetrated my mind; Stan had once again been abducted. I began to panic. Questions flooded my mind in quick succession. *What do I do? Should I call a doctor? Should I put him into the shower? Should I fix him a snack? What do I do? How did they take him out of bed without waking me up? Why didn't I wake up to protect him? Who are these aliens? Why did they hurt him?* Once more the need to find courage and conviction to get us through this new nightmare confronted me. Something inside me said, *Okay, Lisa. Pull yourself together. You don't have time to freak out. You need to document this and get him into bed.* Quickly I ran to get a blanket to cover him. I had to get him warm. He recoiled as I approached him.

"It's okay, Honey, it's me," I said. Any remaining fog in my brain cleared instantly as the Certified Nurses Aide in me emerged.

Checking every inch of Stan's body for injuries, every open sore and bruise, I began documenting every detail of his abduction. Like a crime scene investigator I took pictures, notes, and video of everything.

Working quickly and getting Stan into bed was imperative. So dazed was he from his experience, I had to lead him to the bedroom. After laying him down and covering him up, I climbed into bed beside him, wrapping my arms and legs around him. Holding him tightly, I tried to force his violent shivering to subside. Finally, he relaxed enough to fall asleep. I lay awake for the next hour, watching over him as he slept.[1] Stan shares this entire story in his book *Messages*.

It was still dark out at 5:00 AM. I rolled out of bed carefully to let my hubby sleep. As I went about my morning routine, readying myself for work, my thoughts persistently went to the flattened

---

[1] Romanek, *Messages*, 78-82

grass circle next to the garage. I didn't want to go anywhere near it. But I would have to very soon. My car was parked in the detached garage. A shudder ran through me. *I would soon be standing right smack in the middle of the ominous grass anomaly. The scene has to be documented. The evidence collected.*

The time to leave for work had arrived. The thirty-yard dash to the garage, past the apple tree, would only take seconds to traverse. Facing the waiting door, I took a deep breath attempting to slow my racing heartbeat and calm my anxiety. It was as if the darkness beckoned me, taunting me with its mystery, daring me to confront my lifelong fear of what lingered in the shadows. *You can do this, Lisa. Just run! Run and don't look back,* I told myself. Taking another deep breath, flinging open the family room door, I ran. Unlocking the garage door, I rushed inside slamming it behind me, while flipping on the light. Leaping into the van I quickly locked the doors. My pounding heart and throbbing head felt as if they would explode. *Deep breaths, Lisa. You made it.* As I backed out of the garage, the headlights flashed across the flattened circle under the apple tree. Choking back the bile that rose in my throat, I slammed my foot on the accelerator. My only thought—*escape.*

When I arrived at work, I thought my emotions were under control. Within five minutes of beginning my shift, I began to cry. My co-worker noticed the tears and tried to console me, asking what happened to upset me.

"It was just a rough night. Don't worry, I'll be okay," I sniffled. Then she made the mistake of hugging me. The floodgates broke, and sobs erupted. The whole story of Stan's two abductions came pouring out. She kept holding my hand and rubbing my shoulder. "Please don't think I'm crazy. Everything I told you has really happened."

"I don't think you're crazy, Lisa. I'm just worried about your safety." And she hugged me again. It felt good to have someone to talk to about the weird stuff in my life. A weight lifted from my shoulders. Yet, strangely, I felt guilty. I had a place of solace, a nonaligned friend to talk to. Stan didn't.

After work I called Gio, the MUFON investigator. He informed me he was too ill to come to Nebraska to do the investigation. Gio had instructed me via telephone how best to collect and preserve the evidence. My next call was to Heather, relating the details of the previous night's abduction and my need for help. She and another close friend left Denver an hour later. They drove that night, arriving at our house around midnight.

The next morning a post-abduction debriefing with Stan ensued, recording on film the after-effects of his abduction and everything he could recall. Heather and I gathered grass samples and leaves from inside the circle. Some of the leaves and grass in the circle had been burnt. The smell of the burnt leaves reminded me of a candle-scorched jack-o-lantern lid. Crawling on hands and knees we measured the ten-foot circle. Heather and I rounded up supplies: a tape measure, an apple corer, plastic zip-tight bags, permanent marker, and tape. We gathered samples inside the flattened circle and in increments of five, ten, fifteen, and twenty feet from the circle, as Gio's instructions dictated. Our methods were as scientific as our make-do kitchen supplies. The apple corer was a stroke of genius on my part. A dirt core sample one-inch in diameter and five-inches long ensured that we collected a top soil sample, as well as what lay five-inches below the surface. My apple corer method was less damaging to the rental property than Gio's recommended method of digging with a shovel.

Within days of Heather delivering the evidence samples to Gio back in Denver, we received a call from a woman named Nancy. Nancy, a well-known and respected crop circle researcher, became involved in Stan's case after the circle abduction. She coordinated the scientific analysis of the evidence we had collected, from Stan's many abductions. She also taught me the proper way to package samples. "Never ever put samples of any kind in plastic bags. Only use sterile glass containers," she insisted.

Collecting the dirt as evidence reminded me of how muddied my life was becoming. What began as a fairytale wedding had turned into a mudslinging with Stan. My fairytale "Happily Ever After" now more closely resembled a gremlin-infested fable. Tears welled in my eyes, running unheeded down my cheeks and nose, softly dripped into the dirt. Sobs racked my body as I remained bent to my task, collecting samples. I silently screamed at the intruders of our marriage. *Who the hell are you? What have you done with my husband?*

Stan had changed, no longer was he the loving, sweet, attentive man I married. In his place, an emotionally withdrawn and angry man who had injected himself into my daily life. Love and laughter had been replaced by anger, fear, resentment, and sadness. I was at a loss to understand this drastically abrupt transformation.

I had been married to Stan for five months. After the recent abduction there was now no intimacy between us. The very idea of a sexual relationship was so frightening to him that he would throw up. It didn't make me feel good to have my new husband want to vomit if I became too affectionate. I was trying to accept that the violation by the extraterrestrials had caused some deep subconscious wounds that were causing him to react so strongly. But, I couldn't help but think it had something to do with me, or perhaps it had something to do with the woman in his abduction. It seemed his strongest memory of the abduction was a woman with dark hair. And his need to find her, at all cost. Every time I tried to have a conversation about my feelings it would turn into an argument.

"I'm really hurt that you can't hug or kiss me, let alone make love to me anymore. It makes me feel like you don't love me," I said.

"It's not my fault. Just thinking about sex scares the hell out of me," was his reply. "I have been through a lot, and a little understanding would be nice."

"I'm trying to be understanding, Stan, but I didn't cause this fear, so why am I being punished for it?"

"Lisa, I can only do the best that I can do," he yelled.

My deepest, darkest fear was of the woman Stan remembered seeing with him during his abduction. The jealous part of me, told me that she had more to do with his rejection of me than the ETs abuse did. He was obsessed with finding her. She was always on his mind, and he searched for her face in every crowd and every store we entered. I needed reassurance that he wasn't going to trade me in for the woman he sought—if he ever found her—and that he loved only me. I wanted to be his obsession; I was his new wife for Christ sake….

I told myself repeatedly that everything would be okay, eventually. The recent abduction, the circle in the yard, and Stan's anger were constant reminders that everything was not okay. I needed a break from being the strong wife—who had to be loving, understanding, and supportive. All I wanted to do was scream out my anger and cry out my pain and frustration.

I threw myself a hum-dinger of a pity party that lasted for months. Complete with temper tantrums, anger, self-pity, blame, and tears. Wearing my emotions outwardly, rationalizing that they were hidden, was my greatest guise, even to myself. Unconsciously, I waved my hurt, anger, and frustration like a banner to anyone who would give me comfort, show me sympathy, bestow understanding, and just let me be angry.

Becoming numbly methodical in my daily dealings with my husband and his abductions was the only way I felt our marriage, and my heart, would survive. My repeated attempts to physically show Stan that I loved him, even with a simple hug, was for him a reminder of the aliens' abuse—extraction of sperm through electrocution methods. As hard as I tried to understand, it didn't stop me from trying to pull him back to the here and now, to us, to our marriage. As the months ticked slowly by, I finally gave up. My walls of self-protection were erected. I stopped hugging him and I stopped telling him that I loved him. I couldn't endure the pain of rejection any longer. Whenever he said, "I love you," I would repeat the words, walk away and cry, alone. In tandem with my gradual withdrawal, Stan created an invisible wall around himself, preventing anyone from getting too close, especially me. If I tried to cross that hidden barrier, even to question why he couldn't hug me, he would become so angry that he would say hurtful things and threaten to leave me. His fear and frustration ran that deep.

But certainly, he wasn't the only one putting walls up. I wasn't allowing myself to give Stan what he desperately needed: the reassurance that I loved him, regardless of his repeated rejections, hurtful words, and anger. I wasn't really numb inside, my heart was breaking. The loneliness and rejection was a fire that consumed my every waking thought. It fueled my anger at the aliens as well as toward Stan. I just wanted to be loved, held, and reassured that I was as important as all of this ET/UFO crap seemed to be.

I wanted to be his obsession.

Life at this time was similar to having a beehive in the living room. My protection was in not saying the words "I love you," and it was in not initiating any sort of physical contact with my husband—not poking the beehive with a stick. As long as I didn't disturb the hive, the bees wouldn't sting me. The temptation, however, was the honey inside—the wanting to be loved, the need for the physical contact with the man I loved more than myself. It was ever-present—teasing me to come closer. The trick was to ignore the buzzing altogether.

What I thought was a selfish act of retaliation towards Stan for his inability to make me the most important thing in his life was actually a self-preservation practice. By denying my own negative emotional responses and not creating situations that I knew would cause me emotional distress, I effectively created peace of mind for myself. Peace of mind requires the development of an attitude of emotional and mental detachment to certain situations, which I discovered is vital for overcoming anger. It protects against being too affected by what people think, say, or do. Detachment, I have learned, is not an attitude of indifference or lack of sensitivity. It is an attitude of common sense and inner strength that leads to peace of mind.

This act of detachment, or perhaps I should call it the "art of detachment," allowed me to subconsciously separate myself from feeling hurt. It afforded me the ability to get the emotions under control, to exorcise them, and eventually come to peace with it all. Easy as it is to say, this was not a quick process. Weeks turned into months and months turned into years. Time's never on your side when you need to be, of course. But finally I got it.

I finally understood that everything that needed to be said between Stan and I, had been said a million times. I had to stop trying to force Stan to get back to normal—to the way he was before the trauma of his second abduction. I had to accept that he could never forget what had happened to him. He was no longer the man that I had married. Life's drama and traumas had changed him; much like it does to all of us. This was who he was now, and this was his new normal. I had to stop missing the Stan from the past, the Stan that I married, and start loving the man that he had become. Our future laid before us, and I loved my husband…for the wonderful, loving human being that he is.

It took me many years to understand that doing our best is all that any of us can do. This understanding helped me unlock a hidden secret, one that is so obvious that most people miss the power and importance of it. We are allowed to have our pity parties, to be angry, hurt, sad, and frustrated as long as we are doing our best to understand and resolve these feelings without hurting others in the process. What is the hidden secret that I discovered? It is to live without fear and to love without limit.

***

In spite of the horrible events of Stan's abductions, and our overwhelming emotional turmoil, the holidays were fast approaching. We had to get on with living— or at least pretend that everything was normal, for the kids' sake. We needed an escape from home, to spend time with people who knew nothing about Stan's contact with aliens, to forget our problems if even for a little while. We decided to spend Thanksgiving with my family, in Scandia, Kansas, at my sister's house. My sister's house was filled to the brim with my red-neck, fun-loving family. Their laughter and jokes bolstered our spirits.

Stan's injured ribs were still wrapped and had been explained away as a sleepwalking injury. The details of the story that we told that afternoon were true…minus the part about the abduction.

"What did you do to fracture your rib?" my sister asked.

"I don't know what happened. I just woke up in the back yard, under an apple tree. I must have been sleepwalking or something. I don't remember going outside, or how I got hurt."

Snickering from across the table drew my attention to my brother. *Oh lord, here we go.* I knew from the twinkle in his eyes that my little brother's orneriness was going to be the death of my husband.

"What happened, Stan, did ya get a 'lil too frisky with the knothole in the apple tree?" my brother asked.

"Shut the hell up," Stan replied. His chuckles mixed with groans as he clutched his side. "Don't make me laugh, it hurts my ribs."

Over the next five hours, an onslaught of lewd and colorful jokes ensued with the sole intention of making Stan laugh. It was wonderful to be surrounded by laughter again, and to talk about normal, everyday events.

My only hope was that the laughter would follow us home, and last into New Year's. Fall's golden beauty faded and winter arrived, blanketing our yard with snow. The circle by the garage was finally hidden, no longer a visual reminder of what had happened weeks earlier.

The kids were ecstatic; they could make snowmen and have snowball fights. The flurry of running feet was always followed by the roar of chatter as the kids rushed to find their annual winter uniforms: boots, hats, gloves, and coats. Soon the house would be silent. When I checked on the kids, I found them building a snowman on the very spot where the circle was, next to the garage. The place of fear was now filled with my children's happy laughter, and a scarf-wearing snowman with an orange marker for a nose, branches from for arms, and rocks for his mouth and eyes.

"Do you like him, Mommy?" the kids asked, dancing around their creation.

"I love it, he is perfect."

"Do you think Stan will like him? We made it so he wouldn't be mad about the dead grass anymore."

"I think he is going to love it. Who's ready for hot cocoa?"

"I am! Me too! Wait for me!" came a chorus of excited squeals. I had to move out of the way quickly as three freezing kids came rushing up the deck steps into the family room, and began stripping off wet cold clothes in front of the fireplace.

Christmas was wonderful. Mark and Ann came to visit, and Heather had sent them with a truck load of presents, too. Stan was happy, the happiest I had seen him in months. He had his best friend and his sister with him for the holidays. All I could assume was that he felt safe. When Mark and Ann departed for Denver after our New Year celebration, he was sad to see them leave, or perhaps some part of him wanted to go with them…I didn't ask.

The kids had just returned home from spending a few days with their dad and celebrating Christmas with his family. Christmas break was nearly over for the kids, so they wanted to make the most of it. Stan, the kids, and I played board games, watched movies, laughed, and enjoyed being a family for the first time in months. Again I hoped that this harmony and serenity would last. It felt good to be…to be.

On January 5, 2003 at 4:00 in the morning, as I slept snuggled in my husband's arms, warm and happy, my hope for a lasting peace and tranquility was suddenly and violently ripped out of my grasp. My world spun out of control. Nothing made sense.

7

Mad Mom

Stan woke me up flinging himself all over our bed. As was my usual habit, I waited to see what would happen next. *He must have had another nightmare.* Stan began whispering and shaking me. "They took Jake. I think they took Jake. Lisa, wake up." He sounded really scared.

"I'm already awake, Stan. Calm down, it was probably just a dream," I answered back. I tried to make sense out of what he was saying as he told me about his dream. In Stan's "dream," he remembered four strange looking children holding my son by the arms and trying to drag him through a brightly lit hole in our living room wall. Jake was screaming, "Leave me alone, leave me alone. Mommy, help me. Make them stop. Stan, make them go away." Stan said that he tried to help but couldn't move his legs to run to him. Jake was crying and thrashing to get loose. That is when he woke from the "dream."[1] Doubts began to creep in as to whether it was a dream. I remembered Deborah (Stan's hypnotherapist) had

---

[1] Romanek, *Messages*, 84

told me that my children would not be involved with the aliens because they were not related to Stan.

"Stan you need to go check on Jake," I urged. "You're not going to feel better about this unless you see him in his bed for yourself." Stan ambled off to check on Jake and returned scratching his head.

"That's weird. He's in bed, but he is lying there staring, not blinking."

"He probably heard you come in and opened his eyes," I said, "but didn't wake up completely and then went back to sleep. Kids do that sometimes." We went back to sleep knowing that Jake was still in his bed safe and sound.

That morning on my way to the bathroom, I peeked through the cracked door of Jake's room. He was still sleeping. I shuffled off to the kitchen and made coffee. Comforted in the knowledge that Jake was okay, but still a bit flustered over Stan's dream. I went out onto the deck to smoke and have my coffee. Stan came out a while later and made some comments about the chalk drawings the kids had made on the sidewalk the day before.

After chatting for a bit, Stan turned and asked me, "What the hell is that on our window?"

I looked where Stan was pointing and saw a small equation written on our bedroom window. It could not be seen from inside our bedroom because the mini blinds were down. I panicked. All I could think about was Stan's dream about Jake. I ran into the house and charged into Jake's room like an enraged mother bear. *Calm down, Lisa, you don't want to wake him up.* Getting myself under control, I pulled back the covers and examined Jake for wounds like those Stan had previously returned with. Stan, in the meantime, marched to our bedroom to examine the writing on the window.

I frantically searched Jake's body as carefully as possible trying not to wake him up in the process. Though I could see nothing on him as far as a wound, black permanent marker covered his hands, and erratic smudges splayed across the sheets at the midsection of his bed. But no magic marker could be found. My mind was racing a million miles an hour. Jake did not have any injuries, and was sleeping peacefully. As I started to think about what Stan had told me about his dream of Jake's abduction, a feeling of apprehension washed over me. My confused mind flooded with questions. *Was Jake taken? Was it only a dream? If he was abducted, what had the aliens done to my son? What right do they have to take him?* Fear of not knowing was making it hard to breathe. Every breath I inhaled seemed to catch in my lungs. Something compelled me to turn around and once I did, it took everything I had not to scream. Fear had now transformed to terror.

"Oh…my…*gawd*," I choked. An equation was scrawled on my son's wall. It was in his handwriting. I stood frozen in place for a few minutes. I knew in that instant that Stan's dream had actually happened. I ran across the hall for Stan.

"Grab the digital camera," I snapped between sniffles. "There's writing on Jake's wall. I want to get it cleaned off before Jake wakes up. Those bastards abducted my son."

"What are you talking about?"

"It was not a dream, Stan. They took Jake last night, and he wrote an equation on his wall," I said through gritted teeth.

"You're kidding me. Why would they take Jake?"

"I don't know Stan," But I am mad as hell right now. Just help me, so I can clean up the wall. Maybe Jake won't remember anything, and we won't have to talk about it." Stan stopped asking me questions. He must have felt my anger being directed at him. As we quickly and quietly photographed the equation written on the wall, Jake woke up

"I didn't do that, " he said in a hoarse whisper. "Burglars came into my room to steal my Mountain Dew. They must have done it."

My son was eight years old at the time, and suffered a learning disability. At this point in his schooling he was struggling with addition and subtraction, let alone being able to write an equation like the two now scribbled across his wall.

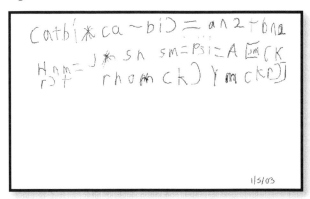

I wrote the equations on a piece of paper, and asked Jake to copy it from the paper—not copy it from the wall—to see if the handwriting matched. It did.

$(a +bi)*(a-bi) =a^2+b^2$

The above formula is an algebraic equation using imaginary numbers, and definitely not taught in third grade math but in advanced algebra in high school. The letter "*i*" is a symbol for what is called an imaginary, indicating the square root of minus one. No one in the house, including me and Stan, knew anything of imaginary numbers, let alone little Jake who attended remedial classes. The other impossible factor in this equation is the use of mathematical carats ($^$). Only those experienced in computer programming use this to symbolize exponentiation. I can assure you, neither my third grader nor anyone in the entire family tree knew a whit about computer programming. The second equation was even more unexplainable.

$Hnm = J^* Sn Sm = Psi = A [Jm (Kr) + rhom (K) Ym (Kr)]$

A physicist and a mathematician could not determine the actual meaning of the equation. They did agree that "Bessel function equivalency" (whatever that means) was the strongest case. Other components of the equation include what is called a "psi function," as well as what is known in mathematics as "Ptolemy's theorem". These Bessel components are used in physics and mathematics to describe behavior of cylinder functions or cylindrical harmonics. You add to that Ptolemy's theorem and you specifically have the behavior of a rhomboid (a four-sided figure) within the confines of a circle or cylinder. This is not unlike the configuration of a door-like figure within a wormhole. Which is what the Orion's talked about in the pictures and equations that Stan himself wrote,[2] describing how they time travel from Orion to here.

Bessel functions, carats, and Ptolemy's theorem? Even after these things were explained they still sound like gibberish to me. I

---

[2] Romanek, *Messages*, 74, 119

don't care which way you look at it, there is no way my third-grade boy could remotely dream up these equations.

"It's okay, Jake," I reassured. "It doesn't matter who did it. I will wash it off so that we don't have to worry about it."

April and Nicole woke up amidst all of the commotion. They couldn't understand what was going on any more than Jake could. I used the excuse that Stan had, on many occasions, written stuff like this, and that perhaps he was sleepwalking again (that was always our cover story with the kids—sleepwalking). They didn't buy it. They had seen Jake's handwriting and knew who had done it. Using my Mom influence I told the girls, "It doesn't matter who wrote it, it's just another weird thing that we can't explain. Let's not talk about it."

Nicci objected. "Yeah, but Mom, why did Jake do that?"

"I don't know, Honey. Let's just pretend it didn't happen. Jake is really scared about the dream with the burglars."

April was not so willing to let it go. "Why is it okay for Jake or Stan to write on the wall, but when I did it I got into trouble?" I could see her point, but without explaining the whole story about the ETs to them, I simply didn't have an answer.

As the girls left, rage began to consume me. How dare these intruders touch my son! How dare they abduct him and use him to make a point to Stan. My husband needed to accept that his experiences with the extraterrestrials were real; that was the point they were trying to make. I was sure of it. The abduction of my son was like an alien wakeup call, as if to say, "You're not dreaming Stan. We are real and here is your proof." Stan had to quit denying his own experiences and deal with the horrifying fact that everyone in the family was being affected.

I stood in my son's room with a bottle of rubbing alcohol in one hand and a rag in the other, seething with anger. My mind screamed, *it is Stan's fault Jake was abducted.* I was hoping that the alcohol would remove the strange writing from the wall, and erase the memory of this event from Jake's mind. As infuriated as I was with the aliens, I couldn't do anything to them, except yell and make threats to the air to never touch my son again. In the chaos that overwhelmed my mind, Stan was the closest person to these alien bastards that I could lash out at. I felt justified in blaming him. *How dare they mess with my son!* Thank God Jake didn't remember what had happened during the abduction.

But Stan remembered. He had tried to save Jake from the hands of the aliens and had failed. As their stepdad, he had taken on the role of the hero—the slayer of dragons and boogeymen. He had, on many occasions, bravely fought off the scary closet dwellers, and valiantly slayed the multitude of unseen creatures under the beds—dust bunnies. His perceived failure and guilt consumed him.

I called Heather and told her what had happened, sobbing through my story. She told me she would leave immediately, coming once again to my rescue. She loved the kids and would do anything to distract them from all of the turmoil. We love Heather. She goes above and beyond the call of friendship—and Heather's husband as well, for allowing her to leave Denver for Nebraska at the drop of a hat.

I then called Deborah.

"Hi Deborah. It's Lisa Romanek. I have a question for you," I began to sob.

"Lisa? What happened?" she asked. "Calm down and tell me what is going on."

"You said the aliens wouldn't bother my children!" I screamed. She was surprised by my outburst. I was usually pretty well-balanced with this stuff.

"Did something happen to the kids?" she asked.

I couldn't calm down. The gates I had in place had finally broken open with months of pent up anger and frustrations pouring out. I bawled, and yelled, and tried to tell her what had happened during the night. About Stan's dream and about the writing on the wall.

"This is fascinating," Deborah said. "Jake is not related to Stan. I wonder why they took him."

"Deborah, you said that my kids wouldn't be involved like this," I snapped again.

"I am sorry. In situations like this where a person is being abducted, the extraterrestrials usually don't abduct non-related people who are in the same house," she said. I hadn't caught the "they usually don't" in our previous conversation. She understood that I was upset and rightly so. After talking for awhile I began to calm down.

"I think it was a message from the ETs to show Stan that Jake could be involved if he refuses to believe and start talking about his experience," I stated.

"What makes you think that it was a message for Stan?" Deborah queried.

"I am not sure why or how I came to this conclusion, but it seems to make the most sense. It's like the knowledge was put into my mind, to reassure me that when Stan accepts the truth, Jake will no longer be involved," I tried to explain. I thanked her for listening and apologized for screaming at her.

Now, my concern was how I would to keep track of Jake and Stan through the nights. I learned quickly that no matter how close you sleep to someone, you can't stop abductions. They happen regardless of your efforts. It was my responsibility as a mother and wife to protect them, and I felt like I was failing. After whatever tolerance and support I had shown to Stan's experiences, the fact that my son was now involved replaced tolerance and understanding with outrage.

I started to ask questions. I started searching for answers. *What makes this abduction thing okay?* Well, some people say that those who have been abducted agreed to it, but most people that I have talked to have no recollection of this. The way I saw it, unless the person had a conscious memory of an agreement, then it was against their will. Abductions are not okay! Period.

Why are abductions happening? I asked myself. The speculations vary, and at best are guesses. I learned that some races of the ETs are working with our government. In my search for an answer to this question, I read the book, *Above Black: Project Preserve Destiny*,[3] written by Dan Sherman. Dan trained in the US Air Force to be an electronic intelligence specialist and later an "Intuitive Communicator." Project Preserve Destiny (PPD) was an alien/military program that Dan was assigned to without prior knowledge of the program. Sherman explains in his book that his involvement in this project began after his mother had been abducted by aliens in 1960 as well as 1963. His PPD Captain told him that random tests were being

---

[3] Dan Sherman, *Above Black: Project Preserve Destiny*, (Wilsonville, OR: OneTeam Pub, 2001)

conducted on the general populace to determine compatibility for "genetic management."

The genetic management phase of this program ended in March of 1968, according to Dan. He also explains in the book that many individuals underwent genetic management while still in their mothers' wombs. His own intuitive communication skill was a direct result of this manipulation.[4] Dan's PPD assignment involved daily communication with two extraterrestrials over a three-year period, as part of the US military's preparation, "for a future time in which all electronic communications would be useless." His PPD job related directly to the NSA (National Security Agency). Toward the end of Dan's communications with his alien contacts, he determined that it was possible he had been receiving communications for ongoing human abductions. "Abductee potentiality for recall, residual pain level, nerve response and body normalization,"[5] were among some of the information that was being received by him. This to me was sounding more like military involvement with abductions than ET involvement. I began to wonder if the military was abducting people as well, while making it look like the ETs were responsible for all abductions. Is that why our government is denying the existence of extraterrestrials? It would make sense. What better way to know what the ETs were changing in people than to do their own experiments on them; throwing these poor individuals into the middle of a ping-pong abduction game between our military elite and extraterrestrial visitors. Are they back engineering humans as well as technology? Perhaps they are doing their own genetic alterations on humans

---

[4] www.projectcamelot.org/dan_sherman.html

[5] Sherman, *Above Black: Project Preserve Destiny*, 132

to create an unquestioning military or an elite force with amazing genetic abilities.

Dan relates, "I finally came to the conclusion, after reporting over twenty apparent abduction scenarios, that I wanted no part of the program any longer."[6] It's important that we have whistleblowers like Dan Sherman to let us know what our military is involved in. For people like me, his story confirmed my darkest suspicions. It is important that people like Dan demonstrate a sense of morality and good consciousness. These programs must be stopped!

I had been angry with the aliens and with Stan for Jake's abduction. Now there was a possibility that our military, who was supposed to protect us from threats like this, was in cahoots with the aliens.

Is it morally right for our government to hide the truth of their involvement with the extraterrestrials? Why is the government allowing men, women, and children of this planet to be abducted, genetically altered, injured, and scared out of their wits? Why is my husband being abducted? Why is my son being taken?

Though my son didn't remember the details of his abduction, he was terrified. He began gathering every extra pillow he could find in the house and put them on his bed. Stan and I wondered what in the world he was doing with all of the pillows. We followed him to his room after about the third trip to the closet that contained guest pillows.

"Why do you need so many pillows?" I asked Jake.

"I need them so that the burglars won't find me again."

I had to leave the room for a few minutes, my throat closing up with emotion. I knew tears would soon follow. I wanted my son to *be* safe. If pillows would make him *feel* safe then so be it. He

---

[6] Sherman, 134

could have all of the pillows he wanted. Stan on the other hand had a problem with Jake having all of the extra pillows.

"This is just silly," Stan snapped at me. "He doesn't need this many pillows." Stan proceeded to remove the pillows from Jake's bed. "Jake you can't have all of these. Put them back where you got them!"

He began shoving the pillows at Jake. I grabbed them from Stan's hands, and put them back on the bed.

"Jake, go outside and play for a little bit. It will be okay, don't worry." Jake ran outside crying because he had been yelled at. "Stop it, Stan! You need to leave him alone. Jake is afraid. Of all people, Stan, I would think you could understand his fear. Stop making fun of him for it. He is an eight-year-old little boy who is scared out of his wits. Why do you have to say it's silly and belittle the situation?"

"Do you still live under the impression that you can protect him or any of us, by simply deluding yourself that you are the only one they are after, or the only one that can be used to do their bidding? I think that was the point of involving Jake. To prove to you that if you won't do what they ask, they will involve us all. Stop making a joke out of this, and start taking it seriously."

"That's ridiculous, Lisa, I'm not making fun of him. I know how serious this is, and I feel bad enough about bringing this weird shit into your lives. I don't need anyone or anything reminding me of it every day. I go to sleep every night worried that I will be abducted. Now I have to worry about the rest of you, too."

"So, Jake having all of the pillows is making you feel guilty? Pillows have, in your mind, become a daily slap in the face—a reminder that you can't protect us?"

"Just stop, Lisa. It's all too much. I can't deal with it."

"You can't deal with it, Stan, or you *won't* deal with it? I have to deal with it every time you are abducted, and now I have to worry about the kids as well. The luxury of ignoring it and hoping it will go away isn't a possibility for me, so why do you feel that you should be afforded that luxury?"

"You need to face the fact that this is happening, that it can't be stopped, and that you should figure out what it is you're supposed to be doing. Pull your head out of the damn sand. Stop trying to control everyone and everything just because you feel your life is out of your control."

"Whatever!" he yelled, hands thrown up in the air.

"Jake doesn't have someone sleeping next to him at night. You do. I am your pillows—your security blanket. All I ask is that you stop removing the pillows. Let him be."

This battle over the pillows waged for months between Stan, Jake, and me. Stan finally gave up the battle because I wouldn't back down in my fighting to protect my son at all cost, even if that protection was simply symbolic or seemed silly. Nevertheless, Jake began sleeping with twelve pillows every night to make a fort so that he would be safe. I was always scared to death he would suffocate inside his fort, but he had a process that he went through every night of putting them in just the right places. Jake could sleep, that was all that mattered.

Stan remained blind to Jake's fear, his own anxiety of abduction was so powerful and encompassing that it was all he could allow himself to focus on.

One morning Jake told me, "Mommy, I had a really bad dream about aliens."

"Really, what did the aliens look like, Jake?" I asked curiously. I tried not to show any emotion that would make him think it was anything but a bad dream. I clasped my shaking hands in my lap so Jake wouldn't notice how upset I was about our conversation.

"They had big blue eyes, with a horn or hose or something out of the front of their faces."

"How big were they? Were they bigger than you?" I questioned. I began clamping my teeth together now to keep myself from grabbing him and again searching his body for injuries. I knew I had to remain calm and not overreact, but it was difficult.

"No, they were shorter than me," he replied.

"Really. Well, do you remember what happened in your dream?" I asked.

"Nope, I just remember seeing them. They were strange looking. I don't like aliens."

Then he ran outside to play. That was the end of the conversation. He wouldn't give a lot of details about them, and I didn't try to pry it out of him. If he wanted to tell me, I would listen. Would he be abducted again? Would the girls become involved as well? That was one of my greatest personal terrors. All I could do was pray that my terror would not become a reality.

8

Closets of Our Own Making

After Jake's experience with the ETs, I began night vigils to watch over Stan, Jake, and the girls. I felt a need to protect them, to keep the extraterrestrial boogeyman away. Jake, April, Stan, and Nicole had suddenly developed a fear of closets and perceived monsters/ aliens coming out of them at night. They began hearing noises coming from inside the closets at night. As with any phobia, the rationale behind a fear is based on the perceiver. Because the kids heard noises coming from inside the closet, they were fearful of what was lurking inside. In our house the talk of UFOs, along with Jake's experience, probably played a major role in the fear that aliens or monsters would get them if the closets were not closed.

Stan's fear of closets was another story. Why would an adult man develop a fear of something so childish? I was no better, though. Look at me: I'm scared of vampires, for goodness sake. How illogical is that at the age of thirty-four? We had both searched the closets when the kids had become terrified and found nothing there. Was Stan's fear based on his own childlike openness? Were they all able to detect something that I wasn't? Many experiencers have reported this same fear. The theory that aliens use closets as gateways was not common knowledge to any of us.

Parents around the world confront their children's fear of monsters in the closet or boogeymen under the bed. But it's easier when you *know* there aren't monsters in the closet, or boogeymen under beds. What do you do when answers don't come so easy? As a spouse, what could I do to reassure Stan? As parents, how do we reassure and comfort our children? Do we search under the bed or in the closet to prove to them that nothing is there? In doing so, are we acknowledging that there might actually be monsters? Opinions by professionals vary; some say to play along with the child's fear and eliminate the monsters with such things as monster spray (air freshener), while others say don't play into the fear of your children; it only reinforces their fear. How can so many professionals disagree on such an important issue? The one thing they agree on is that monsters aren't real. I disagree wholeheartedly with the professionals about the existence of monsters, or what children recognize as monsters.

Many abductees, contactees, and experiencers believe they are visited by aliens when children. Most report memories of first visitations at around four or five years old. Interestingly enough, that is when the fear of monsters begins as well. Of course, the professionals like to put the blame on things such as beginning school or separation anxiety. Here is my advice: listen to your children's concerns and acknowledge these concerns for what the child thinks they are. Ask them what will make them feel safe at night. Empower them. Whether it's a night light, a flash light, monster spray, the blocking of closet doors with heavy objects or twelve pillows, let your kids have them. What is it hurting? Let the child set the rules for this. Just keep them talking about what's scaring them. The same rules apply to spouses like Stan. Listen and provide comfort but encourage them to confront the fear, like an adult.

My children and Stan have eliminated their fear of closets in an ingenious way. There are no closet doors in our home. They have all been removed. The kids have created an illusion of sorts by filling the open closet area with dressers and entertainment centers as well as clothes. They have effectively eliminated the possibility of anyone or anything hiding in that space.

Not all closets are physical, however. We all have closets…a place we hide all of our secret thoughts, fears, emotions, and bad deeds done by and against us—our skeletons in the closet. It becomes easier to hide our fear than to deal with it. The fear of not being able to protect my family from an intelligence I didn't understand was one of those skeletons, knocking to be let out, leaving me powerless. The bones were rattling, mocking me, daring me to try to regain my power. Night after night I sat in the dark, waiting and watching. I didn't find peace of mind, just more fear.

It seems that the more I sat waiting for something bad to happen, the worse the fear became and the more negativity ruled my life. I was creating what I was thinking and feeling by creating more fear, instead of dispelling it. So, I was left with this question: How do I confront my fear without creating more? If I had been given a choice, I wouldn't have dealt with them at all. But as it happened, I was forced to deal with my fear sooner than I had expected.

Two weeks had passed since Jake's abduction, and it was my ex's weekend to have the kids. I couldn't protect them if they were three hours away. Regardless of my fear and my need to keep them safely out of the reach of the aliens, I had to drive them to their dad's house. Twilight had settled into night as we traversed the last thirty miles of our trip.

"Hey look at that, Lisa. Do you see those three lights?" Stan asked. Frustration and anger washed over me. "They're UFOs," he continued. "Holy cow, pull over so we can see them." I adamantly refused to pull over to the side of the road.

"You can see them just fine without my pulling over, Stan. I don't want the kids involved in this, and you know that," I whispered to him. I was trying to keep them ignorant of the UFO aspect of our lives. The kids scrambled to the passenger side of the van, alerted to the possibility of seeing a UFO. Fortunately, the event only lasted about three minutes, and the excitement died out quickly. We arrived at their dad's house twenty minutes later.

"Okay, give me hugs and kisses. Be good and have fun. I love you guys. I'll see you on Sunday. Have fun with your dad. Lock the doors and call Granny," I said.

They shut the apartment door, and I waited to hear the lock click into place. When I didn't hear it I yelled through the door, "Lock the door!" I could hear three pair of feet running back to the door, and the lock finally clicked. "Thank you," I hollered through the door.

The small voices could be heard yelling back, exaggeratingly drawing out each word, "Youuuuu're...welllllllcome." The little stinkers knew I wouldn't leave until the door was locked. I felt guilty for leaving the kids unprotected.

Maybe I should call and at least tell their dad to watch over them while they sleep because aliens had followed us. But how could I tell him that we had all seen a UFO and that it knew where the kids were. It was then that I realized how crazy I sounded, how foolish I had been acting. As I climbed into the van, fear for my children's safety washed over me and I began to cry. With each tear that rolled down my face, the fear eased and rational thought emerged. *They are going to be fine. They are safe. Positive thoughts bring positive outcomes, whereas negative thoughts bring negativity into your life.* Somehow I knew this to be true. The challenge however, is not in believing it, but in knowing it to be true, and living it.

***

Before leaving town Stan and I stopped for gas. While Stan was filling the tank, I strolled into the gas station to get a cup of coffee. As I approached the counter with my loot of snacks and coffee for the ride home, I glanced out the window toward Stan. Stan skittered behind the gas pump with the nozzle flinging wildly in his hand.

"What on earth is he doing now?" I asked, rolling my eyes at the clerk. "My husband is such a nut ball sometimes."

The station attendant leaned over the counter to have a quick look as Stan ran to the front of the van and then to the back of the van, peering around the corners as if he were looking for a way of escape. The attendant began to chuckle.

"I think you're right. What's wrong with him?" he laughed. We stood there watching as Stan flattened himself against the van peering over the hood and ducking out of sight towards the ground. "Does he think he's a double-O secret agent or something?" He asked. We walked toward the door still watching Stan's bizarre antics just as he made a break for it, running full bore for the building.

"Move, get back...shut the door," Stan yelled. The clerk grabbed my arm, pulling me to safety as Stan scrambled haphazardly in the door, pressing his back against it to force it closed. "Holy shit! Did you hear that horrible screaming? Something's out there. I swear it sounds like demons ripping through the earth and screaming up from hell."

As we all moved closer to the windows to peer into the blackness of the night searching for the evil thing lurking in the darkness, Stan vehemently warned, "Don't go out there." To anyone outside watching the three of us, I'm sure we resembled the three wise monkeys. Me, with my hand to my eyes (see no evil) peering to see out of the bright room into the darkness, the attendant with his hand to his mouth (speak no evil) covering the giggles, and Stan with his hands covering his ears (hear no evil.) Stan's trepidation flared up again. "Oh, my *gawd*, there it is again!"

"Where, Stan?" I asked, pressing my hands and face to the window again. "I don't see anything."

"Did you hear that...oh, my *gawd*...what is that?" Listening intently, recognition of Stan's evil screaming sound finally hit me. Like an explosion of thunder, my laughter rang loudly through the convenience store.

"Oh my *gosh*. Stan, is that what you're afraid of?" That's all I could say. Between peals of laughter and gasps of breath I tried to reassure him that his life was not in danger. "It's okay, don't worry." The blank expression of confusion dominated Stan's face. Tears ran down my face as I continued to laugh. Stan was obviously not from around these parts.

"What's so damn funny?" Stan stuttered in his state of confusion. His anger was growing quickly.

"Not evil," I chortled again between gales of amusement. "Stan, it's hogs," I finally managed to sputter. I had never witnessed anyone react to hogs like that before, nor had I considered that the hogs could be the cause of his panic.

"No, it's not! Hogs make an *oinking* sound!" he demanded.

"Okay, maybe on TV, but not when they're mad." Stan didn't believe me. "Come on you goofball, I'll show you." I took his hand and led him outside. Fearfully he followed. I showed him the stock trailer that was parked by the diesel pumps on the other side of the station. "Now do you believe me?" I asked.

"Good Lord, that scared the crap out of me," Stan burst out laughing. We paid for the gas and coffee, and headed down the highway towards home.

After we were on the road for almost an hour, he said, "Lisa, I have the *hee-bee-gee-bees.*"

"Perhaps you are still shook up about the hogs," I said, my giggles flooding the van. We had turned onto Interstate 80 heading west. I was searching the sky behind us, just in case something was following us. I was relieved to see nothing was there. But as I turned to look at Stan, I jumped back against my seat. I was surprised to see the three red lights were back, just past Stan's head out the driver-side window.

"Oh, my *gawd*, look, look, look!" I tend to say things in three's when I am excited. They hovered very low to the ground in a triangular pattern. They seemed to be stationary in the sky but stayed right beside us, so they must have been moving. As I watched, the lights then lined up in a straight line slanting toward the west. It reminded me of Orion's Belt. As I continued watching, the bottom two lights switched positions in a line that again reminded me of Orion's Belt. Forty-five seconds to a minute later, the lights just blinked out. After the craft disappeared, Stan and I fell silent; each contemplating what had just happened.

We had two sighting within hours of each other. Within moments I had etched every detail of this amazing event to memory. Fear took over, but not of something "unidentified." My instinct trumped my rational mind. We had just witnessed three alien craft. *Is this a precursor to another abduction?* I wondered. As Stan and I exchanged opinions about what had just occurred, dread set in. We had to go home. We had to go to bed. And we had to hope that they wouldn't follow us.

***

A week later, on February 19, 2003, Stan and I were sitting out on the deck, enjoying the unusually warm night air, talking about how strange life was turning out for all of us. Stan wandered across the backyard, toward where the flattened circle had been. Our conversation was about the odd red UFO lights we had seen in the sky.

"Stan, do you think my theory is sound? Do you think the craft were trying to give us a message? Do you think the aliens were trying to tell us that you were confused about where they are from in Orion's Belt?"

"I don't know, this whole thing is confusing," Stan said.

As I was looking up at the sky, thinking about this theory and how it seemed to be connected to Orion's Belt, I suddenly jerked in my chair. There were three black triangular craft, silently flying toward our house from the southwest.

"Stan, look, look, look!" I yelled, pointing at the sky. The massive triangular craft must have been pretty close. The lights of the city backlit the low clouds behind all three. They slowly and silently glided northeast over the house and then they were gone. We were shocked, but strangely not afraid.

My theory regarding Orion's Belt stemmed from messages given to Stan during his first abduction. During his experience, Stan asked the female ET where they came from. She put an image into his mind in the form of an answer. The image that Stan recalled and wrote down was of Orion's Belt in the constellation Orion with the star Mintaka circled. My theory was partially correct. It was the wrong star. Stan later asked for clarification during another experience and was told that where they are from is six light years behind the leftmost star Alnitak. This information was further explained during Stan's second regression with Leo Sprinkle, many years later.[1]

> We are...by a planet...we are...six light years down and off from...where you call...(slowly) Alnitak...Alnitak... Alnitak.
>
> Zeta, Orion...pyramid Khufu...Alnitak...we are behind Alnitak and off from your view. We are six light years behind what you call "Orion," on the other side of that. We are...we have a view of...horse...you ride them...word...(slowly) horses head...nebula.
>
> You cannot see it...we have view of Horsehead Nebula.

Events that defied our understanding were constantly taking place. The first four months of the year had already been terrifying with Jake's abduction in January. On February 12th, we saw six UFOs in one night. Three while taking the kids to their dad's house and

---

[1] Stan Romanek, *The Orion Regressions*, (Colorado: Etherean, LLC, 2012) p. 67-68

three more on our way home. Then we had three black triangular crafts fly over the house on February 19th, two triangular crafts on the 22nd, a disk-shaped ship appeared on March 16th, and then, on April 8, 2003, of all things, we suddenly had a *friggin'* "Peeping Tom" on our hands.

Finally, something good happened. A man named Clay Roberts had heard Stan on a radio program and contacted Gio, our MUFON investigator, and got our phone number in Nebraska. Clay wanted to make a documentary about Stan's experiences. We agreed to work with Clay, so he traveled to Nebraska and we signed a contract.

When the "Peeping Tom" showed up, however, the ET stuff stopped. Our attention for the next three months was on catching the pervert in the act. At first we thought it was an isolated incident, and called the police to report it. The police couldn't help us; they had real bad guys to catch, so we were left to our own devices. We began trying to capture the window-peeper so we could present him to the police. That didn't work out well, but I'm sure that the neighbors or anyone who was watching thought we were crazy as loons. We set up traps to tangle, trip, or detain the sneaky peeper. We needed a way to slow him down so we could at least get a look at where he went so we could follow him. There were never any footprints, or signs that anyone had been under the windows that we glimpsed him looking into.

We were beginning to think we were just imagining the whole situation. That is until one night, outside the kitchen window, we saw him looking in again. Stan ran out the front door and I out the back, both circling the house from different sides to capture the little freak. No one was there, but a log had been placed under the kitchen window. The reason for the log made sense; the window sill was seven feet from the ground. I was thrilled, the log validated that we were not imagining it. The fact that we could not run fast enough to even see this person, let alone catch him in the act, was very frustrating.

Stan caught the "Peeping Tom" on July, 17, 2003. Not physically, however. He set up his video camera after catching a glimpse of him outside the dining room window. Stan had realized that chasing him was pointless, so he figured that this would be the next best thing; proof for the police that the face in our window had been harassing us for months, and needed to be captured.

I had gone to bed and Stan and the kids finished watching a late movie on cable. Stan went to the kitchen to get a glass of water before coming to bed. He saw something move out of the corner of his eye, watching him through the kitchen window. Looking out he saw no one. Rushing to the closet in the family room, he retrieved his video camera, and set it up in the dining room. Leaving the lights off, he set it up, turned on the night shot option, and announced loudly that he was going to bed. He then went to the bathroom, and, leaving the door open, he waited to see what would happen.

Two flashes of blinding light from outside the window illuminated the dining room and flooded the hallway that led to our bedrooms and bathroom. Like a little boy trying to catch a peek of Santa Claus, he tiptoed into the hall, flattening his body against the wall, and peered into the darkness. Adrenaline coursed through his body as he crept forward. And in the window, staring back at him was a face.

Stan stopped dead in his tracks and blinked his eyes a couple of times, thinking the darkness of the room and the moonlight were playing tricks on his vision. Keeping his eyes locked on the "Peeping Tom" he rushed past the camera and straight to the window. The face ducked out of sight. Peering out below the window revealed nothing, but movement to his left caught his attention. A kid was running towards the backyard. As the kid ran towards the backyard, he glanced over his shoulder to see if Stan was pursuing him, and ran smack into the bushes that lined the north side of the yard. It being only three days from a full moon, the prowler was bathed in moonlight, which allowed Stan watched his retreat. That is when Stan got a good look at the culprit. His huge black eyes reflected the moon beams while his frail, gangly naked body was illuminated. The sight scared the hell out of Stan.

"Oh, ohhhh, ohhhh my *gawd*!" he squealed as he ran from the window, down the hall and into our bedroom. "Lisa, wake up! Oh, my *gawd*, wake up! I caught him! You aren't going to believe this, Lisa!" he yelled, shaking me out of my peaceful slumber.

"Damn it, Stan. What now?"

"I caught him. Get up, you have to see this!"

"Caught who? What in the hell are you talking about?"

"The peeping Tom, I caught him on tape. Get up!" he said pulling the blanket off me.

"Oh Lord, I am sick of trying to catch that little jerk, just let me go back to sleep, please."

"He *isn't human*, Lisa. I have the whole thing on tape, get up. You've got to see this."

Begrudgingly, I crawled out of my nice warm bed as Stan grabbed my hand and began pulling me down the hallway. I could feel his hand shaking with a combination of excitement and fear. He stopped next to the camera and turned it off.

"Stay here for a minute." Inching slowly to the window, he looked out into the moonlit yard, first left then right. "Whew, no one's out there."

"Can we get on with this, so I can go back to bed?"

Stan flipped on the light and came back to the tripod, rewound the tape and hit the play button. We stood hunched over, cheek to cheek, watching the small view screen. Minutes ticked by, and I saw nothing but the window in the view screen.

"What am I looking for Stan? I don't see anything."

"I don't know. I was hiding in the bathroom. There were two flashes of light, and then I snuck out to see what had caused them. That's when I saw him looking in the window at me."

"How long was this thing running before you saw the flashes?"

"I'm not sure. It didn't seem like very long." Another five minutes of watching the screen finally revealed the first flash, two minutes later the second. The minutes were ticking by. A round bulbous object rose from the bottom ledge of the windowsill. Inch by inch it came into view.

"Holy cow, Stan. Do you see that?

"I told you. I told you I caught him on tape. It's not human." Huge black eyes stared at us through the viewer screen. "Did you see that Lisa?" His eyes twinkled. "The IR [Infrared] from the night shot bounced off his retinas. Where did he go?"

"I don't...he ducked down...there he is again."

"Boo." Photo taken from video by Stan Romanek.

"Holy shit, no one is going to believe this. Where did he go this time? There I am. That's when I saw him looking in the window."

"Shhhh," I snapped.

"I caught you this time you little bastard," I heard Stan's voice boom from the recorder. I continued to watch the viewer as Stan approached the window and looked out. I heard his squeamish cry, "'Oh, ohhhh, ohhhh my *gawd!*'" All I could do was laugh. In the video, Stan was running away from the window, his fear more than obvious as he skittered sideways across the dining room, squealing like a little girl. If the video wouldn't arouse fear or ridicule or both in most people, it would be a definite winning video for *Funniest Home Videos*. I laughed until tears ran down my face.

"Stan, rewind it. I have to see it again." As the tape began to play again, Stan fast forwarded it to the flashes, so we could see the ET who had caused so much fear and frustration over the past three months. "He's not scary, Stan. He's actually kind of cute. Look at how he just looks around the room. Holy smokes, his eyes blink! Did you see that?"

"You're right, his eyes are blinking. But as far as not being scary, you didn't see him running away. I did. If you saw it, like I did, it would have scared the crap out of you, too."

"He looks like he is playing a game of peek-a-boo. Let's name him Boo," I giggled.

We had the proof we needed for the police, but we couldn't show them. We had to hide the tape, and never let anyone except our friends see it. It was truly amazing, it was proof that a life form—someone or thing from another world—was visiting Earth; Kearney, Nebraska; and our family home.

***

On September 5, 2003 Clay and Deborah came to visit. After the visit from Boo, our infamous "Peeping Tom," Clay had insisted on buying surveillance cameras and traveling from Denver to install them.

"Who knows what is going on around your house that you aren't even aware of," Clay said. "This way you can watch the monitors safely from inside the house instead of running outside at every noise you hear."

"That's a great idea, especially now," I mumbled.

"Why do you say that, Lisa?"

"I have noticed a strange pattern with Stan's abductions, Clay. They seemed to happen only in the fall. His first abduction happened in September of 2001, the second happened in November of 2002. It's September, and if I'm correct he will be taken again soon. Maybe we'll catch it on the surveillance."

"That would be awesome. Live footage for the documentary."

I didn't have to wait long for my suspicion to be validated. In the early hours, long before dawn on October 8, 2003, Stan was indeed taken again. This time he found himself lying on the deck naked. His first thought was to cover himself. Tiptoeing around the side of the house, he discovered the garage door unlocked. Rummaging around, he found several plastic bags of the kid's clothes I had gotten ready for the Goodwill. He dumped one of the bags and made pants out of it. Stan woke me up, again banging on the bedroom window.

"What the hell are you doing out there? And what are you wearing?"

"I don't know, I woke up on the deck and the red UFO was flying away," Stan said.

"Where did you get that black diaper?" I giggled. I know this was a serious situation, but can you imagine waking up with your husband or wife, outside during the night, knocking to be let into the house, and finding them wearing a black plastic trash bag diaper pulled up to their chest? Well…welcome to my world! I tried to hide my giggles behind my hand but couldn't help but laugh.[2]

"I'm sorry, Stan, I don't mean to laugh, but you look silly," I said.

He kind of chuckled, "I know, but I was naked, outside! Thank *gawd* someone forgot to lock the garage."

Stan began to calm down a little from his ordeal. We suddenly remembered the surveillance cameras that we had installed were running, and that maybe they had gotten some proof on the tape. We got the tape out of the recorder that was set up in the family room, and immediately put it into the VCR attached to the TV. It had been running for quite awhile, so we fast forwarded it until we noticed a bright light outside the house. We rewound it to minutes before the light and began to watch it. We heard what sounded like a young boy's voice calling out, "Mom…Mom, Mooooom," then a series of beeping sounds. Suddenly a huge circle of light hit the ground.

"What the hell?! Can you hear that Stan? It sounds like Jakey yelling, 'Mom…Mom…Mom.' They better not have messed with my son again."[3]

Fuming with anger, I ran to my son's room. Through the glow of the night light I could see Jake was safe and sound in his bed, tucked safely within his pillow cave. I checked on the girls as well;

---

[2] Romanek, *Messages*, 104

[3] Romanek, *Messages*, 105

they too were accounted for. The uncertainty I felt about the source of the voice prompted us to have voice analysis done seven months later to compare the kids' voices against that of the recording. Jake's voice was very similar, but not a match. *Were the aliens using Jake's voice pattern to draw Stan out of the house?* I wondered. Whatever transpired, I was relieved to know my kids had not been directly involved.

I was becoming angrier by the day. I no longer felt safe in our home. We had to get away from this place, as fast as possible. The paranoid feeling of being watched was no longer an unreasonable suspicion. It was a reality that was being tossed into our faces, with a what-are-you-going-to-do-about-it attitude. I had been married to Stan for a year and a half and were about to move for the second time. Moving was really hard on all of us, especially the kids. April and Nicci didn't have to change schools this time, but Jake did, now that we lived on the outskirts of town. I felt bad for them, but I felt that I needed to try to keep them safe. For two months, peace and quiet reigned until one dark, cold night.

I woke up coughing uncontrollably. I could not understand what had caused such a fit, but it was making my lungs hurt from the exertion. I finally got out of bed and stumbled to the kitchen to get a glass of water.

"Good Lord, what's wrong with me?" I wondered aloud. I didn't have a cold. As I entered the bedroom again, and went around to my side of the bed Stan started talking to me.

"Did they take you, too?" he asked. I laughed at the absurdity of his question.

"Yep they took me, too," I sassed, and climbed into bed and scooted down into the covers. I was still laughing. *What the hell was he dreaming about, now? 'Did they take you, too?'...sheesh, what a goofball.* Stan said he needed a drink of water and to go pee, so he got up and headed for the door.

"What the hell?" he said suddenly. "What is this? Lisa, is this yours?"

"Is what mine, Stan?"

"Tell me this is yours."

"Stan I can't see in the dark. Is what mine?" I snapped. I could hear the panic in Stan's voice, and even in the dark I knew something was wrong.

He repeated his last statement to me. "Tell me it's yours."

"Stan, I still can't see in the dark. Is *what* mine?" At that moment Stan flipped on the bedroom light, and we both got our first look at what the problem was. Stan was standing in the middle of our bedroom wearing a woman's red flannel nightgown, with Mickey Mouse on the pocket. Bursting into laughter, I finally answered his question, "Nope, that's not my nightgown, though it's kind of cute."

I didn't think anything could be funnier than finding my husband in the trash bag diaper. Laughter was robbing me of my ability to breathe and I nearly toppled off the bed backwards. He couldn't help but join me. But it wasn't long before Stan's laughter suddenly changed from smiles to tears and sobbing. I had to calm down and help him. I went into my automatic post-abduction mode. I had to document everything. I had to call Clay and Nancy. *What time is it in Denver if it is 1:30 a.m. here? It is 12:30 a.m. there. And what time is it in Massachusetts? Oh, who cares what time it is! Just call someone. They are going to laugh their butts off over this one.*

Stan got me to snap out of the laughter and thoughts that were running through my head.

"Oh, my *gawd* Lisa, help me get this damn thing off. There is something on the back of it."

"What do you mean there is something on it?"

"I don't know what it is, but it is cold and wet. It must have been stuck to my back...Oh *gawd*...that is disgusting. Help me, don't...oh, don't get it on my head, yuck, hurry...pull it straight up." Stan's whole body was convulsing in disgust at the thought of the unknown wet goo that was sticking to him.[4]

"Stan, shut up already. Sit down so I can reach you." I had to pull quite a bit with his wiggling all over the place. It was still hard not to laugh, but I was trying. He is such a girl sometimes.

Stan noticed I was still coughing. "Lisa do you remember them doing anything to you?"

"No, I never do," I replied.

"Well I do, they were putting something down your throat. I don't know if it was before they took me or after I was back, but I remember it as clear as day."

"Well, that may explain the horrible coughing spell I had," I said. What I *did* remember that night stopped my laughter as quickly as it came. I remember seeing the red light coming into our bedroom window in the middle of the night. I remember Stan waking me up to see the light, talking about it shining through the window, discussing what it might be, then Stan getting out of bed, and then nothing. Nothing until I woke up coughing. The roof of my mouth began to sting as I ran my tongue across the area. I found what felt like a small cut. "Look at this and tell me what it is." I pointed to where it hurt and opened my mouth really wide.

"That is weird. It looks like a half-moon-shaped scratch," He said. We documented all of the injuries, called Clay and Nancy, put

---

[4] Romanek, *Messages*, 122-123

the foreign nightgown in a sealed container, and went back to bed. *Well, that blows my theory about Stan's abductions only happening in the fall, I thought. It's Valentine's Day…and just another normal abduction night at the Romanek house.*

So many things had happened over the past year that it would be hard to talk about everything. Something strange seemed to happen on a weekly basis. We really liked our new home, but we had started talking about moving to Colorado. We were trying to run from the weirdness that was invading our lives. Black SUVs were now following us everywhere we went. *No, it's not paranoia*, I had to tell myself. *They really are following us.* Stan had a very odd encounter with a woman in a black SUV while walking around our neighborhood. She stopped on the side of the street, and waved to Stan to come closer so she could ask him something. Stan assumed she was lost and needed directions, so he approached the vehicle.

"Hi, can I help you with something?"

She just looked at him and stated, "If they [our scientific investigators] want to get it right, they have to re-evaluate the Rosen Bridge [wormhole theory]."

Stan didn't understand what she had said. "Huh? What is a rosenbag?"

She repeated it for him, "If they want to get it right, they have to re-evaluate the Rosen Bridge." She rolled up her window and drove away, leaving Stan standing in the street totally confused.

When I got home from work, he was telling April and I about it when all of the sudden he yelled, "Holy crap, there she is again! She's outside by the mailbox. I have to get my camera. If I get a picture, then…you'll believe me."

Where in the heck is his brain? Instead of seeing what she's doing by our mailbox, he wants to take her picture…so that we…will believe him. He began running haphazardly through the house. Dodging, ducking, and weaving around furniture, through doorways, and bouncing off walls in his rush to retrieve the camera. *Are all men this spastic?* I wondered. *Or is it just my goofy husband?* April and I wanted to get a good look at the woman in the SUV, so being calm and rational females, and for some reason smarter than *some* members of the opposite sex, we simply walked to the window to see her. There was no need for the camera in our opinions. If he wanted to prove she was real, all we had to do was look and see it for ourselves.

"Stan, she's driving away."

"Damn it, I missed her. What was she doing?" He asked.

"I think she put something into the mailbox," I said.

"What if it's a bomb?" he asked.

"Good, Lord, are you kidding me Stan? Why would she give you a message today and then put a bomb in the mailbox?" I said laughing. "Go see what it is."

"I'm not going to go look. Are you kidding me? It could be dangerous!" Stan yelled.

"You are all crazy," April said. "I'll go see what it is, ya big scaredy cats." April marched out to the mailbox, expecting to find nothing, and came back carrying a letter. "That is so weird," she said. "Why would she put a letter in our mailbox? It just says Stan and Lisa on it." She handed me the envelope.

As I started to open it, Stan freaked out, "What if it has anthrax on it?"

I scolded him, "Would you stop talking like that? Good, Lord! It is probably from a neighbor or something." I opened the envelope and inside was a card. As I read it, my smile faded and I went into a momentary state of shock, letting the card drop to the floor.

"Good luck on your move to Colorado," it said. "And remember, we are watching!"

No one knew we were moving yet. No one!

At this point in my life, I realized I had to make a choice. Do I make a stand against unknown forces, or do I try to hide from those forces? The woman had effectively flung the doors to my closet wide open, and an avalanche of junk came tumbling out. Somehow, I was buried at the bottom of the pile. I felt suffocated by the weight of all of it. I had a choice to make…should I stuff all that crap back into the closet, or sort it all out and get rid of what I didn't need? I had been hiding in the closet among my physical and emotional traumas, doubts fear, and guilt for so many years that I had become my own monster.

When the initial shock wore off, I realized the card was validation that we had not imagined being followed. We were indeed being watched. *I can throw out the fear of insanity. I'm no longer afraid of the ETs, so I can get rid of that, too.* Piece by piece I tossed away the excess baggage. I evaluated what remained: anger at the ETs for invading our lives; guilt for not being able to protect my family; fear of the humans who I now knew were watching us; frustration that we were again being forced to run and hide from the unknown and the unwanted presences in our lives. We moved to Colorado Springs, Colorado two months later. And though we thought the past two years had been terrifying at times, it would turn out to be a walk in the park compared to what we were about to experience.

9

Dangerous Move

All hell broke loose. Someone broke into our house. This was no ordinary break-in. Nothing of monetary value had been taken. It was glaringly obvious that it was perpetrated to steal one specific item: the UFO file, which contained copies of documentation of the past abductions. Some of which was in digital form, and other physical papers. A pall of disbelief and apprehension hung like a shadow over our serene cul-de-sac neighborhood—over my family.

The kids had been home alone when the robber had entered the front door. Stan and I arrived fifteen minutes later. The kids had gotten out of the house safely. They then decided to booby-trap the house in an attempt to seal the individual inside.

"Oh, my *gawd*, you could have been hurt!" I yelled. "What if the intruder had caught you, and hurt you?" I was more scared than mad but I was yelling nonetheless. "Don't you ever do that again! Do you understand? If someone comes into the house you get to the neighbor's as fast as you can, and call the police. Is that understood?" I asked as I hugged them. "You kids stay here. Stan and I will go check the house."

This is crazy, I thought. *Most moms are warning their kids not to play with matches or to stay out of the street. I am lecturing my kids not to capture burglars.*

Cautiously, Stan and I checked every closet, under beds, and behind curtains. No one was inside. The only thing missing was Stan's UFO file. We found the empty folder tossed to the floor, partially under the bed. I told the kids it was safe to come back inside. They did their own search to be sure we had not missed the intruder hiding somewhere.

Stan called the police to report the break in. When the officer arrived we told him that personal files had been taken but did not tell him it was Stan's UFO stuff. The officer took the report and recommended that we watch our credit and accounts for identity theft. He then pulled Stan and me aside and proceeded to tell us that he thought the kids had made the whole thing up. He accused the children of taking the file themselves. I was furious. My kids had been really scared. They could have been hurt, and he acted as if it was nothing to worry about.

Our friend Heather had warned us not to move to Colorado Springs because there were so many military bases. In a way, I had felt comfort in knowing there were so many military bases so close to our house; maybe the ETs wouldn't bother us anymore. Her warning had fallen on deaf ears. We didn't care if there were military bases in Colorado Springs, they had nothing to do with us. We were more concerned about whoever had been watching us in Nebraska.

The card had said, "Good luck on your move to Colorado. And remember, we will be watching." Was this part of that warning? Did this break-in have something to do with the military? Who in the military would want to harm us? I was tired of looking over my shoulder all of the time wondering if we would see the familiar black vehicles following us. I knew we had to be cautious. Why did they enter our home in the middle of the day? I was tired of being afraid and running from every shadow. Now I was afraid to leave the kids home alone.

Stan's biggest concern was about his missing UFO file. He was so obsessed with getting the answers to why he was being abducted, he had thought of little else for the past three years. This behavior and lack of interest in me, or anything non-ET related, was putting a major strain on our marriage and our family. It was hard for me to watch Stan struggle to come to terms with his abductions. I guess I kind of understand what he was going through. There were a lot of unanswered questions, and Stan had the answers safely locked away in his subconscious mind.

It was time to tell the kids the whole story about Stan and his experiences with UFOs and aliens. We needed them to understand how serious this was. It was now affecting all of us. I didn't want to scare them but there was no other way. They had to know the whole truth. The girls' reaction was expected; they didn't want anyone to know. They were afraid if their friends found out they would be made fun of and would be teased about being crazy. I understood their fear. I was battling that feeling as well. We all were. Jake seemed to take it in stride. He opened up and began talking to me about his own abduction.

"It was aliens that came to my room, Mommy. I didn't want to tell you 'cuz I thought you and Stan would be mad at me, and say I was lying," Jake confessed. It saddens me that my child had to deal with the emotional turmoil of his abduction alone. He had been afraid I would be mad at him. I wanted to protect him from the truth, and had isolated him in the process. Stan, as an adult, could barely deal with his abductions. Plus, he had me to talk to. As I sat hugging Jake, I began to cry, and so did he. He was still so afraid, but now he had me to talk to.

"It's okay, Jakey," I soothed. "You don't ever have to keep secrets from me. If something happens that scares you—you come talk to me, I won't be mad, I promise."

The girls walked away, shaking their heads. "You guys are crazy. Aliens aren't real," April announced. "Please don't let our friends know." And so began the battle of truths, even within our own family.

***

Stan and I attended the 2005 MUFON (Mutual UFO Network) Conference in Denver. Phyllis Budinger was to speak at the conference. She is the analytical chemist who did the analysis of the strange metallic substance found in Stan's hand after his second abduction, as well as the nightshirt soaked in the mysterious goo he had been returned in after his fourth abduction. Phyllis was also presenting her analysis of the dress worn by Betty Hill during her 1961 abduction. Before the lecture began, a petite woman approached Stan and me in the lobby.

"Are you Stan Romanek?" she asked.

"Yes." Stan answered.

"I have a strange question to ask you. I don't want you to think I am foolish for asking this, but I need to know. Did you return from an abduction experience wearing a nightgown?" she asked.

"What? Who are you?" Stan asked. His curiosity was tugging at him more than his fear at that moment. He was still suspicious of everyone and everything.

"Oh, I'm sorry, my name is Kathleen. I am Betty Hill's niece." Stan and I were so shocked by the question about the nightgown we didn't know what to say or do. *Could this woman possibly be the owner?* I wondered. *How had she found us? How did she know about the nightgown?* Betty Hill? It took my brain a minute to catch up with what she was telling us. Oh my gosh, this woman was related to Betty Hill.

I heard Stan reply, "Yes I did. How did you know that?"

She didn't answer and instead asked another question of her own. "Was it a red plaid nightgown with a Disney character on the pocket?" Kathleen asked.

"Maybe we should go sit down and have this conversation in private," I suggested. We found a quiet place to talk.

"I believe Betty was abducted shortly before she had passed away last October," Kathleen continued. "Her favorite nightgown was missing, and she was pretty upset about it. Was the nightgown you received as I described it?"

"Yes, it was. Did Betty happen to end up with a t-shirt that said: 'I've been abducted by aliens and all I got was this lousy t-shirt?'" Stan asked.

"I really don't remember, but I wasn't looking for one either," Kathleen said. The lecture was about to begin, so we parted ways and didn't see each other again during that weekend. Stan and I were so surprised we could barely contain this information, but we couldn't tell anyone. There was no proof. We didn't even know if this woman was really Betty Hill's niece. Stan didn't take the woman seriously; he was convinced that the nightgown belonged to the dark-haired mystery woman, whom he remembered being with again, during the nightgown abduction. I found the possibility of the nightgown being Betty Hill's fascinating. The idea was just too fantastic to be plausible. Or was it? It wouldn't be long before we realized that *nothing* can be too fantastic.

Two weeks later, I found a message on our answering machine. I hit the play button and was shocked to hear a mechanical-sounding British woman's voice, with a warning to Stan and myself. After listening to the entire message, I ran to the bedroom and woke Stan immediately to have him listen to it. I was terrified. The voice sounded computer-generated, with a flowing British accent:

> *"Hello Stan and Lisa. My intention is not to scare or alarm you, but to warn you. It is great that you are back in Colorado, but Colorado Springs was not a good idea. It seems you have moved into their backyard. Now it is easy for them to get to you. I know how stubborn you are, Starseed, but please heed this warning and know that Lisa and the children are at risk also. Now listen, Starseed, you know you are different. Follow your instincts and stay alert. This is too important. Soon it will all be revealed and, Starseed, do not be afraid of what you are..."*

"What the hell is a Starseed? And why is she calling me that?" Stan asked.

"I have no idea, Stan. But that is the least of my concerns. I am more worried about her saying the kids and I are at risk also. What in the hell does that mean?!" I shrieked. "That's it. The kids are not walking to the bus stop alone anymore. I don't care if it is only two blocks away. We are in danger, and we don't know from whom! We no longer have control of our own lives. We are puppets for these people to play with, whoever they are. I really hoped we would be safe here. What are we going to do?!"

This was a new type of fear, a fear I had never known. I thought the fear of losing my kids in the custody battle was terrifying. That was like a cakewalk in comparison to this dilemma. Now my children's safety, and possibly their lives, was being threatened.

"We can't move again!" Stan screamed back at me. "We have a lease. What do you want me to do? I don't know how to make this crap stop any more than you do. You said you would never move again, no matter what happened," Stan taunted.

I began to cry. Nothing seemed to change. Stan always seemed so singularly focused about the impact this had on his case; the mounting evidence, the documented proof. I didn't feel that he showed any concern for me and the kids. We began to take our anger out on each other by throwing accusations, placing blame, and never understanding each other's emotions. Was our marriage doomed? Would my family survive this harrowing ordeal without being hurt? Time would be the judge of that.

"Why does everything have to only be about you, Stan? Why can't you see that the kids and I are involved in this also?" I sobbed. "I am scared to death right now for all of our safety, and all you can think about is what 'Starseed' means? Are you kidding me? Do you care about anyone but yourself?" I was sobbing so hard I could barely breathe between sentences. And I am sure Stan couldn't understand most of what I was saying.

"Oh, Baby, don't cry," Stan said pulling me into his arms. "I'm sorry. I'm worried about you and the kids, too. We will find a way to make this all stop. It will be all right. *Shhhh*, don't cry," he soothed.

I just stood there in his arms crying. I wanted my husband to do more than tell me that he cared. I wanted my old, quiet, uneventful life back. I knew things could never be the way they used to be. Too much had happened, and we had all changed. *Well,*

Lisa, you married him for better or for worse! You better learn to deal with the worse because better seems to be taking her sweet time getting here, I thought.

We called Clay to tell him about the automated voice. He told us that he had received a call from the same voice, two weeks earlier. He said that he had decided not to tell us about it right away because he was worried that it would scare us. I was angry with the mystery caller, with Clay, with Stan, with myself, and just about anyone else who crossed my path. I didn't know who was responsible, but God help them if I ever found them. "Clay, if you ever keep information that concerns us a secret again, you will no longer be working with us to do the documentary. Do you understand me?" I snapped. I was furious.

"I'm sorry," Clay muttered. "I really was trying to protect you. I didn't want to upset you. You will understand after you hear the call I got," he said. He played the recording for us, and it was exactly the same mechanical-sounding British voice that was on our answering machine. This part of the recording got my attention:

> *"We look to the day when everything will be revealed; knowing it will be enlightening for all. But there are those in specific agencies that would disagree, and for many reasons, most of which have to do with ego and power. And they are getting aggressive because they are scared of the inevitable..."*

Alejandro Rojas became our investigator in 2006, and when we presented him with the many recorded messages we had received from this British female voice, he began searching for a source. He came across an AT&T Natural Voices Text-to-Speech program named Audrey (UK English) that sounded very similar. However, the text-to-speech program sounded like a program: very robotic and monotonic. The female voice that contacted us had inflections in her speech. The name Audrey stuck, and we could now refer to the voice with a name. Audrey would prove to always be a mystery. But clues gleaned from the communications helped us discern who is responsible for individual calls. Is Audrey working from within the military and trying to help us? The early messages suggest that she is. Is she alien, using the technology to communicate? Strange as it may seem, the more enlightening personal communications suggest that she is extraterrestrial. Could she be a simple program used by Black Ops groups to try to scare and mislead us? As the years have passed, and as the calls continue, we have surmised that this could be the case as well.

The rabbit hole grew that much deeper, and this was no longer an ET-Stan affair. It quickly became clear that other clandestine groups or factions were interested in these experiences as well. Who is watching us, exactly? And how do we know who to trust?

A few days after the Audrey call, my daughter Nicole was taking pictures of the stormy sky with her new digital camera. Stan liked the picture and was going to use it as his computer background. When the picture was adjusted to fit the screen, he noticed a UFO in the picture. The next morning April had borrowed Nicole's camera and went to take pictures, too. When she loaded the pictures on the computer, something startled her.

"What the hell is that?!" Stan and I quickly came to look at the pictures. We couldn't see what had gotten her so upset. "Can't you see it?" she urged. "Step back a little bit and look again." To our surprise, there on the screen was a zoomed-in picture of what looked like a little grey being.

"How did you get a picture like that?" I asked her.

"I didn't take that picture. I found the camera on the floor this morning and went outside to take some pictures." She said.

It was as if a little ET had come into our home in the night, picked up Nicole's camera, and accidentally taken a couple pictures of itself. We jokingly named him "Curious George" because he was curious about the camera, and kind of cute like a monkey. I thought, *Christ, what next? Not only do we have human intruders making their presence known in our house, but now we're dealing with snooping aliens, too.*

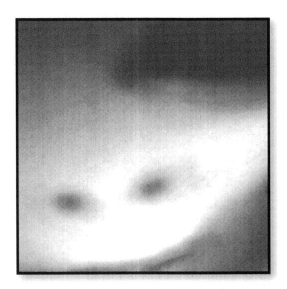

The phone calls, the helicopters, the break-in, the betrayal by friends, and the fear of the Unknowns were starting to drive us over the edge. This is the kind of harassment that the Men in Black and Black Ops are notoriously known for. However, for better or for worse, no Men in Black had ever come knocking on our door. It would have helped us to believe that these events were really happening if they had. We also could have documented actual people telling us to shut up about the experiences with the ETs and UFOs. Instead, they were acting like cowards and perpetrating a one-sided assault that we could not defend ourselves against. Their lurking, watching, and harassment was causing fear and anger. Yet, they were being obvious in their molestation of my family's quietude. Why? It wasn't until we began filing police reports, and Stan began talking to people, including a two-hour interview with the producers of the Peter Jennings special *UFOs — Seeing Is Believing,* that aired in January 2004, that the Black Ops upped their game.

On December 20, 2004 Stan was assaulted by three men in an unmarked black SUV.

Photo by Lisa Romanek.

Black vehicles seemed to be around every time we left the house. Obviously, a new surveillance team had been assigned to us now that we had relocated to Colorado. Sometimes they would be parked outside the house on our street in the cul-de-sac. Sometimes we would notice them parked down the street or across a connecting street. Were they the "white lighters" (as we called them) that seemed to want to help us and warn us of danger, or was it the "dark force" (Black Ops) who wanted to harm and frighten us? Stan actually tried to approach one such vehicle. It was parked in the middle of the street to the south of our house. They were holding up traffic behind them, and it seemed, purposely drawing our attention to them. We had been videotaping the baby foxes next door when they pulled up. I watched them pull up, and told Stan to hold the camera down by his hip and point it in their direction, but to continue to watch the kits play. With the video zoomed in we could hopefully see who they were. They were taking pictures of us with a big camera that had a telephoto lens. As Stan approached the vehicle to within about a few hundred feet, they quickly turned the car around and drove the other way. I felt as though we were bugs placed under a glass to be watched.

With the help of supporters, we had surveillance cameras installed outside of our house again and were recording around the clock. If anyone came close to our house, we would know it. One evening Stan was using the computer and had gotten distracted by something on television that I was watching. He had left the computer on, and when he went back to continue to use it he noticed the screensaver flashing, "YOU CAN'T HIDE." All of the desktop icons had been removed, and none of the software worked. They had all been deleted. I'm not sure how that is possible, but it happened a lot over the next few months. Someone was able to hack into our computer and do it whenever they wanted, deleting important files in the process.

When our milk delivery order sheet was tampered with and stamped, "YOU CAN'T HIDE," we stopped the milk delivery service that same day. The store was just down the street. It wasn't a big inconvenience to stop delivery. I didn't want to take the chance of having our milk and cheese poisoned.

We didn't feel as though we were hiding. As Audrey had said, we were, "living in their backyard." It was psychological torture perpetrated by some insidious faction of the military because of our involvement with the visitors. I think many people are going through the same things we are, and they are just as terrified as we are, feeling like no one's listening.

***

On our way home from a trip to Denver we stopped for some supper at a fast-food hamburger place in Castle Rock, Colorado. We were in the process of ordering when the van died. Stan tried over and over again to get it started to no avail. A few of the employees came out to help us push the car out of the drive-thru and into the parking lot. We had no idea what had happened, it was running fine just minutes before. We found a repair shop close by that was open, and called to have them tow the van. The mechanic looked at it and told us that the computer was fried. He asked if we had been hit by lightning, due to the damage of the electrical system in the van. He said it would take a week or so to get it fixed due to the extent of the damage.

We called Heather, who came to pick us up and take us home to Colorado Springs. When we arrived home we realized that we left the keys to the house with the mechanics. It had been a long day, and we were obviously not thinking clearly and just wanted to go home. We tried to get into the house but all the doors were locked. Then I remembered I had grabbed the garage remote out of the van and put it in my purse. We pulled Heather's car into the garage and when we went into the house the front door was open. As impossible as it seemed, someone was in the house when we had arrived, and had gone out when we pulled into the garage.

The break-ins had become so frequent that fear was a secondary emotion for us. Anger at the invasion of our privacy and our home was first, and then distress took over. We searched the house to make sure no one was hiding, and to see if anything had been stolen. I don't think we even considered what we would do if we actually found someone still in the house. Our instinct was to keep the kids in a secure place, search the house, get them inside and calm them down, call the police, and wait for the next round of attacks from the unknown and unseen invaders. This had become our daily routine—our normal routine. Searching for what they may have left, changed, moved, or taken was never ending. It was a psychological war waged against Stan and I. The calling cards left behind by these individuals made my skin crawl. For example, Dwight Connelly had just given us his book, *The World's Best UFO Cases*, at the 2005 MUFON conference we had recently attended. I had left it on the dining room table, when Stan and I had gone to a movie. When we returned home from the theater we found the book balanced on the light that hung over the table. The book had been creased open to reveal a missing page. Page 227 had been ripped out. The only thing we knew was that it was part of Stan's story that Connelly had included in the book. The next morning I found the missing page tucked into my work uniform.

The drawing of the three beings from Stan's first abduction was the focus of the page. Why had they left us this message? My thought is that they wanted to purposely flaunt the fact that they had once again been in our house, and that there was nothing we could do to stop them.

Drawing by Stan Romanek.

The UFO file was again taken. We had learned to keep a bogus file so that they had something to take when they came snooping. It was almost comical that they repeatedly took the file we set up for them. While unpacking everything from Heather's car into the house, Jake had gone to his room to watch TV.

"Hey, Stan, someone is messing with the cable," Jake yelled. "My TV went all static-y." You can't turn off kids' cartoons and not expect to have chaos break out.

"Jake, I will check the cable as soon as we are finished unloading the car," Stan yelled back up to him.

"No, someone is outside messing with the cable, I can see him," Jake continued to yell. He could see someone out his bedroom window. Stan ran out the back door but the person had already escaped out the gate. Apparently he could hear Jake yelling as well. The cable wires had been cut just twenty feet from where

I had been standing at the dining room table. I called the police to report the vandalism and also report that some (UFO) files had been taken. They said an officer would be there soon. At 10:30 PM, two hours after I had originally called, I called again. I told them I had been waiting for two hours, and that we were tired and going to bed. I asked that they send someone first thing in the morning. An officer came to the house the next morning. He took his report, photographed the damage, and left. We took photos of the officer while he was there to prove that we do indeed call the police to report these happenings.

Photo by Stan Romanek.

We also attain copies of the police reports in case the reports were to disappear from the police department as well. At this point anything was possible. The next day we had Schlage locks installed on all of the doors in the house. For the next couple of weeks the helicopters were around constantly, driving us nuts. We got the van back but still had problems with the electrical system.

We had to take it back a few more times before they fixed all of the damaged areas.

***

On March 5, 2005 a new mystery presented itself. Jake had a couple of his friends spending the night and the three boys had fallen asleep on his bedroom floor watching a movie. The girls and I had gone to bed as well, leaving Stan awake, working on the computer. Stan had fallen asleep in a recliner while waiting for a program to install. The sound of footsteps woke him up and he saw a small naked figure run through the hall towards the kitchen. Thinking my son and his friends were playing a game of Truth or Dare or something, he went to the hall closet and got his camera, intent on capturing the moment as blackmail against Jake when he got older and started dating. With the camera rolling, he searched the kitchen and lower levels of the house. Finding no one, he started up the stairs to Jake's bedroom, narrating the film as he walked. He flung open Jake's door to find three startled, sleepy-eyed boys peering up from the floor at him.

"Were you guys downstairs a few minutes ago?"

"No," a trio of voices responded.

Shaking his head, Stan said goodnight to the boys, and headed back downstairs with his camera still running. It was then that movement outside the sliding glass doors, that lead from the dining room to the backyard, caught his attention. There, crouched on the other side of the door, a wrinkly, pale alien was staring at him through the glass. Stan went ballistic, swearing and running. "Holy shit! What is that?! What the hell is that? Oh, my *gawd*; oh, my *gawd*...what is that thing?!"

The alien slowly sank lower as it backed away into the backyard, disappearing from sight. Seized by fear and utter amazement, Stan ran from the dining room to the kitchen and back to the dining room, all the while looking out the windows trying to see where it went, and too afraid to open the sliding glass door and follow it into the backyard. On his final trip to the kitchen window, a series of flashes erupted in the backyard, drawing Stan's attention. Stan's last uttered words on the video before it went black were, "What the hell was that?"

The video then suddenly continues, forty five minutes later, and you then hear, "I just saw flashes of light outside…I need to calm down. What in the world is going on? Where did those flashes of light come from?" For no particular reason the camera had stopped, and then restarted. Stan had checked the clock in his office when he was looking for the mysterious naked kid, and it was 12:45 a.m. When he, and the video, came to and he started talking about the flashes of light again, the clock read 1:35 a.m. Approximately one hour had elapsed from the time he went up to Jake's room, to seeing the ET, and then seeing the flashes of light. Stan had no memory of seeing the ET, just the flashes of light. It was only after he rewound the tape that he remembered the entire event. He couldn't account for the missing time either. The question remains, however: what happened during the forty five minutes that the camera didn't record?

The video Stan had captured that night, of this little fellow, was remarkable. Contrary to popular belief, not all Greys are grey. This alien was predominantly taupe-colored, like dark coffee with cream, and had hint of blue coloring where his veins protruded slightly across his skin. Seven feet was all that separated Stan from this Grey, staring at each other from opposite ends of my dining room table.

Screen captures of two frames from video taken by Stan Romanek of "Grandpa Grey".

Where Boo (the ET in the window) was *cartoonishly* cute, and George was so darn adorable looking, this Grey we named "Grandpa Grey" did not elicit a humorous or cuddly response. Even from the video, you get the feeling that he was visiting for a reason. No funny business or games with this alien. Perhaps his appearance of being older and wiser set him apart from the others we had seen. Perhaps he was a superior, an Elder, a controller of some kind within the Grey race.

As if the surprise visit from Grandpa Grey wasn't enough to deal with, the mystery deepened the following week. A card arrived in the mail with a document from Schriever Air Force Base inside. The White Lighters were hard at work; they wanted us to be aware of what was really happening. It was awesome to finally feel that we had gotten an answer as to what the hell was going on, and who was involved. The card included a handwritten note on the back of the document.

> *We have gone to great expense getting this to you. Maybe now you believe that you must move. Do not release this to the public or contact anyone involved for your safety and ours.*

The note warned us not to release it to the public, for our safety and for the safety of those who had secretly gotten it out of the Air Force Base. It also reiterated the warning from Audrey that we needed to move out of Colorado Springs. Knowing that everything we had been experiencing while in Colorado Springs was really being perpetrated by clandestine factions of the military was liberating and empowering. We knew who the culprit was. It was not the ETs that we needed to fear, it was the very people whose duty it was to protect us from threats, both foreign and domestic. The United States military!

The most benign question I had after reading this document was how they knew Grandpa Grey would be coming. The document was sent from Air Intelligence Agency Division, Schriever AFB, Co 80912-2116 to "Commander," Office of Special Investigations Department of the Air Force, Pentagon, Washington D.C., February 21, 2005. (Thirteen days before we had the visit from the being we call Grandpa Grey.) It reads:

Project Romanek:

Be advised, we expect Romanek to have a visitor soon. We will try our best not to miss it this time; there [sic] closeness/ proximity is convenient to say the least. Also HPM worked, van incapacitated. But Mr. Romanek is smart and stubborn and has a strong support system. It also seems that he is getting inside help? We will investigate. If Romanek stays at location HPM can be used on residents and parties involved, if available? As you know subject must be in range, we will fallow [sic] up as things unfold.

HPM stands for High Power Microwaves. Eureka Aerospace in Pasadena, California developed a device to be used by police to stop a car during high-speed chases. Since the 1970s, every car is built with some sort of microprocessor-controlled system—like the ignition control and fuel pump, the microprocessor controls a lot of vital car systems. When a two second blast from a HPM device is shot at a vehicle, the electric current affects the wires and leads to a power surge which, in turn, burns out those microprocessors and burns up the wiring in the vehicle. Eureka Aerospace is partially funded by the US military. In effect, the same microwave radiation that reheats pizza in a microwave can be used to fry the electrical systems in cars, stopping them dead in their tracks. The document states that HPM was used to incapacitate our van, and can be used against "residents and parties involved." I assumed "residents" was a misspelling and was supposed to be "residence." In my research of how HPM works, however, I learned that the word "residents" in the document was not a misspelling; it can and is used against people as well.

DEPARTMENT OF THE AIR FORCE
AIR INTELLIGENCE AGENCY

FEB. 22 2005

21 February, 2005

Commander
Office of Special Investigations
Department of the Air Force
Pentagon, Washington D.C.

Project Romanek:

Be advised, we expect Romanek to have a visitor soon. We will try our best not to miss it this time, there closeness/proximity is convenient to say the least. Also HPM worked, van incapacitated. But Mr. Romanek is smart and stubborn and has a strong support system. It also seems that he is getting inside help? We will investigate. If Romanek stays at location HPM can be used on residents and on parties involved, if available? As you know subject must be in range, we will fallow up as things unfold.

Air Intelligence Agency Division
Schriever AFB, CO 80912-2116

Sincerely

Serge███████
Air Intelligence
Schriever AFB, CO
80█████████

Classified by: G-1

1 of 1 Enclosure

Lisa Romanek

U.S. to Use Microwave Weapons On America Citizens

By Lolita C. Baldor
The Associated Press
Tuesday 12 September 2006

Air Force official says nonlethal weapons should be used on people in crowd-control situations.

Washington - Nonlethal weapons such as high-power microwave devices should be used on American citizens in crowd-control situations before they are used on the battlefield, the Air Force secretary said Tuesday.

Domestic use would make it easier to avoid questions in the international community over any possible safety concerns, said Secretary Michael Wynne.

Who the hell do these people think they are, using weapons against United States citizens—against my family? What makes it right to do their experimentation on us to make sure it would be safe to use it during wartime situations, against foreign enemies? *How did my family become the enemy?* I wondered. The malice behind the words was obvious, and as long as we lived in Colorado Springs, we would be sitting ducks—easy targets.

It really was a year that got me about as close to Hell as I'd like to get. Like the previous year, so many things happened during the time we lived in Colorado Springs that it is hard to write about them all. Here is a basic list: Stan's assault, two documented aliens playing in our house, three abductions, three break-ins, four "Audrey calls," one implant, one listening device, our van damaged by high power microwaves (HPM), one military document, computer hacking, and more helicopters than we could count—thanks to the military surveillance and harassment.

142

We were making plans to move again. This time we really felt we were running for our lives. The remaining four months of waiting for our lease to be up seemed like a lifetime. We now knew that running and hiding was not an option. The military, the aliens, and the white lighters always knew where we were. But, we didn't have to make ourselves such easy targets. They had won again. We were running. But they did not break our spirits; we would not give up that easily. We would never stop talking about Stan's experiences—it was too important to Stan, and to the world.

The card that the Schriever AFB document was mailed in had a message. It was a quote: "In their daily lives, all are braver than they know." –Henry David Thoreau.

Bravery is defined as courage in the face of danger, difficulty, or pain. My courage was about to be put to the test on a much more personal level.

10

Who Cares for the Caregiver?

"Lisa, you have a call on line one," a voice sounded over my walkie-talkie.

"Thank you," I responded.

Rushing to the nurse's station, I picked up the receiver, pressing the blinking button and addressing the caller. "Sunrise Center, this is Lisa, how may I help you?"

"Hi, Baby, are you busy?" I knew even before answering the phone that it was going to be Stan. It wasn't intuition, it was routine. He called me at least four times a day. His need to stay in contact with me, even while I was at work, frustrated me but was nothing new. He was always nervous when alone. "Lisa, I think something happened last night. I have a bruise on my arm that has triangle puncture marks in it."

"Hi, Honey. Yes, I am busy. I'm at work. You know I can't deal with this crap right now. Can we talk about this when I get home? I have to get back to work." I always felt horrible for being short with Stan, but being curt was the only way to get him to understand that I couldn't always be available to deal with problems at the drop of a hat.

After Stan's call, I felt the back of my head for a goose egg. No lump, but the pain was unbelievable. *Is there a connection between the marks on Stan's arm and the painful area on my head?* While washing my hair before work, my fingers had brushed an intensely sensitive area on the back of my head. *Holy crap, was I abducted?* I chuckled. *No, absolutely not.* I didn't have memories of anything happening to me the previous night, or any other night for that matter. I wasn't sure how to react. As the day wore on my thoughts became scattered. But the thought that I may be among the many that have been abducted by extraterrestrials was, to be honest, ridiculous. *There is nothing special about me. What possible use would I be to an alien race? My responsibility is to support Stan, right?* Right!

Like most women, wives, and mothers, I pride myself on my proficiency, efficiency, and my preparedness to deal with any situation that confronts me. As the saying goes, the hand that rocks the cradle rules the world. My world revolves around everyone I know, everyone else's stresses, activities, problems, dramas, and traumas. The myriad of responsibilities I take onto myself include my three kids, my ex-husband, parents, friends, siblings, my marriage, work, housework, cooking, and shopping. I balance Stan's emerging illnesses, his near-daily extraterrestrial related experiences, and the ever present threat of the Black Ops and the break-ins. I don't have time to worry about myself, nor would I allow anyone else to.

Stan was waiting for me when I arrived home. "Do you remember anything about last night?" he asked.

"No, I remember going to bed. That's all," I answered.

"Something weird happened last night. I was up late watching TV and you came down from the bedroom and stood at the top of the family room stairs and said, 'You can't get anything done with these helicopters around all of the time.' And then you turned around and went back to bed," he said.

"That is weird, Stan. I don't remember anything. And I need you to look at the back of my head," I told him. "It feels like I hit my head really hard on something, but there isn't a bump." I moved the hair away from the spot that was causing me pain. Stan searched the area with his fingers.

"Oh, my *gawd*. You have a hole in the back of your head."

"What are you talking about? I don't have a hole in my head. Would you please stop poking at it? It hurts like hell," I snapped. That didn't stop him.

"Yes you do, Lisa. And it looks deep enough to stick a tooth pick in it."

"Don't even think about it, buddy. It hurts enough without you trying to see how deep it is. If you're going to take a picture of it, then do it, and stop messing with it." Stan rushed to the hall closet, digging frantically through a box until he found a black light. Closing the drapes to darken the room, he shined the light on the back of my head. The area around the hole in my head glowed in a small triangle shape.

In this picture you can see the hole and the fluorescing under the black light.

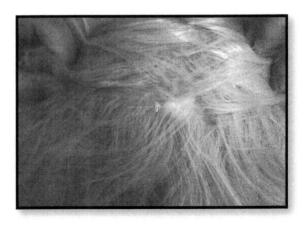

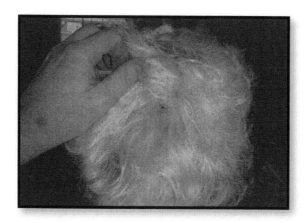

"Oh, my *gawd*, Lisa. I think you were abducted, too!"

"Shut up. I was not abducted."

Denial wasn't working anymore. *Great, now I have what appear to be abduction markings.* That very thought catapulted me out of my comfort zone. And the freak out began.

In the weeks that followed the abduction, my apprehension increased that my friends and family would find out. *Would they all think I had lost touch with reality?* Hell, I was questioning my own mental stability. *Will my bosses question my competence?* Would they continue to trust me to perform by job as a caregiver for the elderly, if they knew the truth? *Just leave it alone, Lisa. You have too much to do, too many other responsibilities that need your attention, you don't have time to worry about this crap. Let it go.* The tactic of denial had worked with dealing with my emotional turmoil in the past, forcing it from my mind. Dealing with my problems at a much later date was my safety valve. Just turn it off, and it didn't exist. But, this…I couldn't let go of. Stan's abductions were a part of my daily life, along with the fear that Jake could once again be taken.

I truly felt like a woman without an island. I had developed some very bad habits many years ago as coping mechanisms, like overeating and smoking cigarettes. Fortunately, alcohol abuse and drugs were never apart of my emotional survival practices. Many people think that the bottom of a liquor bottle provides the relief they need. With me, it was the bottom of an M&M® bag.

By the end of the month, I began sinking into depression. My mind was so overwhelmed with the incessant thoughts about what may have happened to me that the simplest misstep by my family or co-workers would arouse my anger. A torrent of angry words and accusations would pour out of me, simply because a pair of shoes was left in the hall, or a resident hadn't gotten the care that I deemed they needed. Uncontrollable tears and then laughter usually followed the angry outbursts. *Losing one's mind isn't easy. To simply surrender to the stress and fear and allow the depression to rule my life, to sit in a corner and drool like an idiot, seems like a perfect vacation. Holding it all together is a difficult job.*

Heather, my closest friend at the time—savior of my sanity—came to my rescue. Heather had come to visit and, in short order, noticed that I had changed. I was a mirror image of Stan after his abductions began. I was exhibiting the very traits that I had loathed in him. My lack of control of my own life was making me distant, controlling, angry, hateful, and at times hurtful. Heather saw first-hand my angry outbursts, and knew something was terribly wrong. "Lisa, I'm worried about you," she said. "Talk to me. What is going on with you?"

"Nothing is going on. You don't need to worry about me. I'm fine," I said.

"You have never lied to me before, why are you doing so now?" she asked, rubbing my shoulder. *Oh hell,* I thought. *Don't hug me. Don't comfort me. Don't look at me.* And then it happened. Heather took my hand, and led me to the couch. As she forced me to sit, and took the position next to me. "Come on, Lisa, talk to me. What is wrong? You know I think of you as the daughter I never had, right? You can tell me anything," she soothed.

"I know," I whispered. Like a shattered looking glass, I fell to pieces. Sobs and shivers racked my body as the torrent of bottled up emotions spewed forth. "Why would they abduct me? What gives them the right to violate people against their will and wishes? Hell, without their knowledge, without my knowledge?" I said gulping air between broken sentences mixed with near hysterics. A constant flow of words, half of which I think were pure babble. "I can't take any more. Stan, the kids, work, not having enough money to cover the bills, the break-ins, and the abductions. All of it is just too much to deal with. What do you think they did to me? Oh Heather, if they took me, and they abducted Jake, what if they abduct April and Nicci too? I can't save them. What do I do? How do I protect everyone?"

"Shhhh, Lisa, It's okay. You can't worry about *what-if's*. You have to only worry about right now, and take care of yourself. Tell me what you remember," Heather coaxed.

"That's part of the problem, I don't remember anything. How can that be possible? Stan remembers his abductions. Why don't I?"

"Lisa, do you want to know what happened? Do you think it would be easier for you to deal with the reality of your own abduction if you have all of the details? Or would it be more upsetting? The reason the ETs try to erase the memories of abductees is so that they will not live in fear. A lot of repeat abductees don't know that they have ever been abducted. Much like *you*. Do you really think this is the first time you have been abducted?"

"No," I said, taking a deep breath, and letting it out slowly. "I can think of a few of Stan's abductions that I had questions about.

Remember the nightshirt abduction? I woke up coughing from an irritated throat. Stan remembers them putting something down my throat."

"Then let me ask you this, why has this abduction affected you so deeply? What is different from the other times that you question?"

"I had of a hole in the back of my head. What kind of monsters put holes in people's heads? Did they poke something into my brain?" Heather began to laugh, much as I had done to Stan on so many occasions. "Did they put an implant in my head? What did they put in me or take out of me? I've heard stories about extraterrestrials harvesting eggs from women and sperm from men. What if they did something like that? Or, oh *gawd*, or worse yet, do they have sex with women?" Sniffling and wiping tears from my face, I asked, "Why are you laughing?"

"You are under a lot of stress, Lisa. I was laughing at myself. Suddenly, I was thinking that I need to buy you a new pair of shoes. That's what you need." Heather knew I loved shoes, and that was her way of distracting me from my worries, she would buy me something nice.

One by one, Heather and I discussed my questions, and she helped quiet my doubts. Telling Heather my troubles was liberating. Knowing that she was listening and hearing felt wonderful. There is a difference between listening and hearing. Listening is a passive act. Hearing what someone says engages you in a discussion. For the first time in a long time, I was being heard. But I had to give up control in order to do it. My problems, fear, and pain were being brought forward, and I was facing them head on. No more denial. I am a victim of abduction. But I would no longer be a prisoner of fear, or a slave to my own doubts. I had to allow myself to be helped, to let someone care for me for a change.

"Lisa, what are you doing to help yourself? Are you allowing time for just you? Do you allow yourself to enjoy a long relaxing bath or a nap? Naps help you heal."

So, who cares for the caregiver? Well, I suppose it's the caregiver! It begins with ourselves. And when we reach out for help, we will always find a caregiver, a loved one, a friend, a partner, or a spouse who will hear and help heal those fears.

Dwelling on what happened to me during my abductions has never been a priority for me since my conversation with Heather. It simply isn't important for me to know the details, nor to worry about them. I have never undergone regression to search for the details of those experiences, as I don't feel that they would reveal anything of benefit to me. My belief is that I have learned the lessons that my abductions were supposed to teach me: that of wearing the shoes of an abductee, as well as walking the path as a spouse of an abductee.

I would learn much later, though, that there was more to my abduction experiences than I could have ever imagined. I would learn why I was important, and what part I played beyond being Stan's support.

My abduction had roused Stan to question his own memories. It was time to push forward. It was time to know the whole truth, to reveal all of the hidden secrets. What was about to be exposed would make my recent freak out look like a nap in the shade on a hot summer day.

11

Pulling Back the Covers

One of the most terrifying aspects of abduction for a spouse is the hidden truth. Unknown details can be devastating to a marriage. I soon learned revealing them can cause havoc.

"I think I'm ready to do another regression. I need to remember all of what happened to me," Stan announced one afternoon. "I want to know if the flashbacks I have been having are really what happened or if I'm crazy." Stan wasn't the only one who needed answers.

"Are you sure, Stan? I will call Deborah and set it up if you want me to," I assured. "It will be okay. Don't worry. I will be with you this time."

I called Deborah and we agreed to meet to do the session. Stan was really scared. He didn't know if he was really ready to learn the answers he had been so obsessed with.

I needed Stan to get the answers so his preoccupation with the ET stuff would go away. Then maybe we could work on fixing our marriage. I missed my husband. Being roommates and dealing with aliens was not what I had signed on for when I entered into our marriage.

The week of waiting for the meeting proved nerve-wracking. Stan tried to call Deborah to cancel the regression a few times. The fear of what he would learn loomed in front of him, frustrating him with fear of the unknown. Was he ready to acknowledge the truth? Could he face his demons?

I hadn't been present for Stan's first regression, so I was excited to be able to watch the process this time in person. But as I listened to Stan's story unfold under hypnosis, describing what had happened to him during his second abduction, I shook with anger at the violence inflicted on him. I wanted to demand that Deborah stop the session. It was like watching some horror film, and my husband was the lead role. Stan at first appeared calm and relaxed. His demeanor changed suddenly. He began to thrash his hips and torso about in his chair. His hands and feet seemed restrained somehow by invisible shackles. He began to scream, arching his back in agony, crying out for help and begging his abductors to stop the torturous ordeal. *No wonder Stan didn't want to remember,* I thought. *This was why the ETs wouldn't let him remember.*

"They keep messing with me," Stan explained.

"Who are they?" Deb questioned.

"The creatures—the things. I'm on a table. I can't move. And they've got my legs spread. And they're sticking something in me. They've got some kind of metal object; it's strapped around my legs. And it's got tubes. It's almost like I'm being electrocuted."

"Besides these things being strapped to your legs, is there any other part of your body in which it seems to connect?"

"My genitals! They've got something stuck in me. And man, it hurts. It's like a tube from the ceiling and it almost looks like a vacuum. But it's it keeps shocking me, and shocking me, and shocking me, and my whole body down there spasming. They're collecting something. They're taking something from me. I don't know if it's urine, or if it's sperm." The pain of reliving this experience became so unbearable that Deborah moved him to a higher level. He no longer felt the pain or fear, but was able to watch as an observer.

Oh, my gawd, why are they torturing him? Stan was being electrocuted? Is this some form of forced ejaculation to harvest his sperm? Being raised on a farm, I know what husbandry practices are. An electric prod is used to shock the testicles of bulls, hogs, and sheep to cause ejaculation for insemination into the females. *Why would they need his sperm?* What Stan was describing sounded like this same procedure.

Bile rose up in my throat, threatening to gag me. Rage toward these aliens for the cruelty inflicted against my husband caused me to nearly vomit. I sat with my eyes closed, unable to block out the sight of Stan thrashing in pain on Deborah's recliner. Even after covering my ears I could hear him screaming as he relived his memories. My heart ached for what he had endured. *I shouldn't have been so excited to learn what had happened to him. Why did I push him to relive the abduction?* Now I wished I could forget the details like Stan had for years. I would gladly do so. But what I saw, what I heard, what I felt in Deborah's office can never be erased.

As Deborah moved Stan forward in time, he remembered a woman being with him during his fourth abduction. Deborah asked Stan to describe the woman and anything he could remember about her that might be important.

To say I was stunned was an understatement.

Over the last eighteen months Stan had been searching for her, hoping to find her in almost every woman he encountered that fit her description. He knew he would find her, eventually. Fear overwhelmed me because of his obsessive need to find her. What impact would his finding her have on my life, my marriage, my family?

As the regression continued, my fear increased tenfold as Deborah uncovered more memories. *Holy shit,* I thought. *She is real.*

"Now that you're sitting right next to her, can you see her face a little more clearly?" Deborah asked.

"She's got long, kind of curly brown hair. I think she has hazel eyes, maybe brown eyes. It's kind of hard to tell. She's slender, mid to late thirties—early forties. She looks to be my age but she seems to be a lot fitter than I am," Stan said. "She's got an accent. She's scared, she says she's scared. And they're grabbing my hand and it's time to go."

"Who's grabbing your hand?" Deborah asked.

"About four of those little guys," Stan answered, referring to the Greys. "We are led into a room, and we're just sitting there, and then all these little kids come in. I don't know if they're kids— they kind of look like kids. The woman looks real happy. She starts hugging them and then she looks at me and I look at her. We're both really confused. These kids come hug my leg and hold my hand, and it's really weird!"

I looked over at Deborah. She was looking at me as well. She could see the sadness, fear, and shock I was feeling. *She is real.* Over and over it rang in my mind. *She is real.*

I could feel Deb's concern for me like heat from a flame. We were shocked at this strange turn of events. It was that tangible. Astonishment held me suspended in the moment. Nothing was making sense. *She is real.* However, my concern for these children and how they got on the craft with Stan and the woman pulled at my heartstrings. I know they abduct children, like Jake. But why abduct children and then introduce them to strangers? Why so many?

"They're little kids…they're bouncing around playing and laughing and hugging us. I don't think they can talk. Some of them seem to be toddlers but they're smarter than toddlers. And they know us. They know us, they really know us."

I sat there breathless trying not to cry. Stan loves kids. He had already had to deal with losing custody of his own daughter.

"What told you that they seem to know you?"

"Well, the woman seems to know them, and they seem to know her, and they seem to know me. I don't really know how they know me. They seem familiar but I don't understand it. It's weird because the beings are watching us really closely. They're like— almost like they're studying us. It's really bizarre."

"About how many children do there seem to be, if you were to guess by looking?"

"Like, maybe seven. They're all naked. Naked little kids everywhere. Some of them are really adorable—damned cute. But they are weird-looking—they don't look normal. They don't have normal eyes."

"Can you describe what their eyes look like?" Deborah coaxed.

"Yeah, they have big eyes, big blue eyes. There are a couple that have brown, maybe, and kind of Oriental-looking," Stan answered.

"Do they have any whites of their eyes showing?" Deb asked.

"I think so. I was looking at 'em 'cause their heads were a little bigger than they should be. They are different. They're too smart for being that little. The toddlers shouldn't be walking at this point; should be crawling."

"So, if these were regular human children, how old would you say they looked?"

"Maybe one to two years old, all the way up to maybe four."

"I see some emotion on your face, what's causing these emotions?" Deborah asked.

"I've got to go!...I don't want to leave 'em behind," Stan said as he began to cry.

"You don't want to leave who behind?"

"The babies...they're crying! I can see them crying. They're reaching for me and they're making me go! The ETs are taking me away from them." Stan began to sob, the kind of heart wrenching sobs that you feel all the way from your toes. It was so hard to watch him relive this ordeal and not go to him and comfort him. I can't imagine how alone he must have felt while on the craft, surrounded by these small children.

"How do you feel about these children?

"I don't know. I'm confused. I don't want to leave them, though."

Now I had the answer to my earlier question. I now knew why they were taking his sperm. *What on earth is going on? Are these beings creating children? Why did Stan have this experience? Do they belong to Stan? Were these children the product of Stan and that woman? Did they have separate children?* I thought my head would explode with so many thoughts and questions running through my mind.

After the regression ended, Stan sat there as stunned as the rest of us. We had just learned that he had off-world, hybrid children.

And he apparently had a stronger connection with the woman than I had initially thought. He began to tell us more information of what happened on the ship. He tells the rest of the story in his book *Messages*.

To make matters worse for me, Stan began telling Deborah during the regression debriefing how he and the other woman clung to each other on the craft. Again, I sensed Deborah's concern regarding my reaction to this information. How was I supposed to feel about this situation? My emotions wrenched at me, leaving me so jumbled I wasn't sure if I should laugh, cry, scream, or remain silent. I didn't know what was expected of me, what my reaction should be. Deb pulled me aside, wanting to make sure I was alright. "Are you okay, Lisa?"

"Yes, just a little confused. Stan didn't have a choice in the creation of these children nor did the woman. I know that. Being angry at them for what has happened would be silly."

It sounded like a good answer. Years later, I found out how he really felt when I read his book. About how the children were his and the woman's, how he was filled with the feeling of euphoria in his heart. I was devastated. He couldn't share those emotions with me, but he could share them with the world. How could something as horrible as rape lead to feelings of euphoria? I remained silent and put on my poker face and smiled. I reassured Stan that I understood, as rage at his new-found happiness seethed below the surface of my calm.

Once again I hid my true feelings of betrayal, fear, anger, rage, sadness, jealousy, and loneliness behind an outward illusion of comfort, calm, and poise. Again, effectively stuffing all of those emotional monsters into my closet and slamming the door shut. My own abduction, though, had taught me that it was only a matter of time before that closet would no longer stay shut. Eventually I would again have to deal with what was happening in my life. Though I was staying strong and supportive for Stan, I was still not taking care of myself. His feelings became more important than mine. I was his support, he wasn't mine. Silently tormented by my thoughts, paranoia became my outlet. The weird thing about suppressing emotions like this is that the more you try to push them aside, the more you have to deal with them later. Trust me. It's better to deal with them when they happen. If you do, you save your family and your marriage. I would have to learn this lesson the hard way.

12

Paranormal Pranksters

They invaded our new home. We began to hear knockings on the walls and little feet running across the roof. Rocks were thrown at the windows. It seemed they were trying to get our attention. At first it was a little nerve-racking, but I quickly realized that the activity was not malicious. Stan, however, was always afraid when the activity started. He was afraid the ETs were coming to take him again.

Because of the high strangeness that had invaded our house, the girls were having a hard time sleeping at night. Jake still had his mountain of pillows to hide in, and slept soundly. April and Nicci, now sixteen years old, would wake up terrified by what they described as shadow people standing over them, watching them sleep. April and Nicci woke Stan and I up often with their screams for help in the night. Some nights, the girls would see what they described as trolls in the corners of their rooms and on their ceilings. This was far more serious than children being afraid of the boogey-man. At first we thought the kids were having a hard time adjusting to the new house or because we had moved them once again. But they really liked the new house and the new town we had moved to. They were looking forward to school starting so they could make new friends. I really didn't think things could have gotten any stranger.

One night we heard someone moving the deck chairs around, and when we went outside to see what was going on, the chairs had been thrown in the yard off of the five-foot-high deck.

"That's strange, why would someone come into the backyard and throw the chairs off the deck?" Stan asked.

"I don't know. Maybe the neighborhood kids are messing around."

We went down into the yard to retrieve the chairs and sat them back in their original places on the deck. Over the next few nights, the chairs were thrown from the deck a couple more times. We devised a plan. If we heard anything, we both would run out different doors and around the house to cut the little devils off. This plan was sounding rather familiar—like the plan to catch the Peeping Tom alien we named Boo, back in Nebraska. A few nights later, we heard the scuffing of the chairs on the deck again. Stan ran to the deck as I ran out the front door. I didn't see anyone run from the back yard to the front yard. I snuck around the corner of the house. Slowly, I began inching my way in the dark, expecting to have someone jump out at me any second. As I rounded the corner, a huge figure loomed over me. I screamed and started to run when I heard Stan scream as well. "Holy crap, don't scare me like that!" Stan laughed. "I about had a heart attack."

I sighed with relief. "Did you see anyone?"

"No, but the chairs are in the yard again," he chuckled. It didn't dawn on me or Stan that it could be ghosts. I had never heard of ghosts moving objects outside of the house. But if aliens were real then anything was possible, right? Feeling defeated with our attempt to catch the culprits, we went and sat on the deck and laughed about how ridiculous our plan was. We were hearing sounds like someone walking in the yard but we couldn't see anyone. "Shhhh, did you hear that, Lisa?"

"Hear what?" I asked.

"Stay put. I will be right back." He went inside and got the camera. He began snapping pictures of me, the yard, the church yard field behind the house, trying to capture pictures of the pranksters. I decided that I didn't want to stay outside as Stan was taking pictures. I went back inside and watched him from the kitchen window as he wandered the yard lighting up the night with his flash. Stan finally joined me. "I got the hee-bee-gee-bees out there. I can still hear someone walking around but can't see them."

We uploaded the pictures to the computer and were shocked to see the culprits who had thrown the chairs off the deck. They weren't kids at all—at least not from our neighborhood. To our amazement, our chair-throwing pranksters turned out to be a familiar face, to say the least.

I would later find out that this picture is of an alien who calls himself "Grandpa". We had been outside, right there next to them, and saw nothing. What kind of technology could render them invisible and still allow them to move objects? Is it due to the multiple densities that co-exist in the same time-space? Like stepping though an invisible curtain, or looking through a one-way mirror, they can see us but we can't see them? This creature, Grandpa, would later reveal why they were playing these pranks. He said they enjoy watching our reactions to situations that they create. I can only assume it is a form of entertainment for them, much like humans enjoy watching monkeys at the zoo.

"Grandpa Grey" had been right next to us, and we saw nothing. Photo by Stan Romanek.

While sitting alone on the deck one night, I got an unnerving feeling of being watched. I headed back into the house. I didn't want to be outside alone if the aliens who were in the pictures showed up again. I decided not to mention the creepy feeling to Stan. He has a tendency to overreact to every creak and bump in the night. After so many years of dealing with the ETs, I understood that if they wanted to take us, they would, and nothing we could do would stop them. Stan and I went to bed about 15 minutes later. As we laid there talking, we heard what sounded like footsteps on the roof. We jumped out of bed and rushed out onto the deck to catch the little tricksters in the act, only to find the deck chairs gone again. We searched the yard below the deck, but this time they weren't there. As we turned around and headed up the deck steps I spied the missing chairs.

"Stan, I found them…" I said, pointing to the roof. He just shook his head.

"How the hell did they do that so fast?" He asked. The chairs were lined up in a row on the peak of the roof above our bedroom. Stan wanted to get up there and get them down so that the neighbors wouldn't think that we had lost our minds. I told him to leave them there because the roof had frost on it and it wouldn't be safe to get up there. We took pictures just to document the incident, and went back to bed.

Photo by Stan Romanek.

"If you want to impress me," I said to the ETs as I crawled back into bed, "you will put the chairs back on the deck where you got them." On nights like this when feelings of unease had settled over me, my bedtime ritual was to call in the angels for protection. I would ask the Archangel Michael to come, and station angels at every corner of the house, and watch over my family as we slept.

Like the aliens, if the Angels were there I couldn't see them, but I felt safer just thinking that they were watching over my family through the night. The next morning the chairs were still on the roof. Apparently the aliens weren't worried about impressing me.

I had to take the kids to school, so I distracted them as we backed out of the driveway and drove down the street. *They will never know this event has happened,* I thought. When I picked up the kids that afternoon, April told me that a friend at school had asked her why we had chairs on our roof, and she had replied that Stan had strange friends who were probably playing a joke on him. Then she wanted to know why they were really there. I simply told her that she was probably right; Stan's "friends" were playing a joke on him. She rolled her eyes at that and asked that I make sure her friends didn't find out that Stan's "friends" were aliens. April and Nicole were at the age where rejection was forever looming over their heads, and that if anyone knew what Stan was experiencing they surely would not have friends. Jake, on the other hand, thought it was all kind of cool and didn't care who knew about Stan and his UFO sightings and abductions.

Objects continued to be moved, and sometimes thrown inside and outside of the house. We were never going to get away from the high strangeness that was now governing our lives.

One night April woke Stan and me up by bursting into our bedroom.

"Mom, there is something in my room. Can I sleep in here with you and Stan?" she begged. "I was watching TV and I got this creepy feeling that someone was behind me watching me from the hallway. I got up and shut the door and locked it. I think the shadow guy was in my room again. It is the same feeling that I get when I am trying to sleep and I see him standing by my bed." She became so afraid that she bolted upstairs to be with us.

Shadow knocks plant off bookcase. Photo by Stan Romanek.

"Come here, Honey, lay down on the floor next to my bed. Here's a pillow."

"I don't want to sleep on the floor. Can I sleep on the loveseat?"

"Yes, just go to sleep, its 2:00 a.m.," I snapped. April kept talking and I had to tell her to be quiet or go back to her room, which I knew she didn't want to do. *Finally, quiet,* I thought as I started to drift back to sleep. From across the room a thump sounded on the carpet.

"What the hell?" April yelled.

"April, stop. Go to sleep," I scolded her.

"They're throwing things at me now!" she screamed. I jumped out of bed and turned on the closet light to find a candleholder and candle that had been on my dresser now lay strewn across the room, on the floor by the loveseat.

Stan was getting mad, "Tell her to be quiet and go to sleep."

"Stan, go back to sleep and stop being a jerk. She's scared. You of all people should understand how she feels right now. If you don't want to help figure this out then let me deal with it." I then hollered at the pranksters. "Stop throwing my things, you're going to break them!" Whether they were ghosts or ETs, I didn't care. I picked up the candleholder and placed it back on my dresser.

"April, try to ignore it. They are drawing energy from you and are able to move things easier."

All of the sudden, all hell broke loose in the house. Pounding erupted through the walls and the roof along with more throwing of the candles. I yelled at the culprits, "Stop! You are just making me mad."

The chaos subsided. It got eerily quiet.

"Mom, your room is scarier than mine. Can I go sleep in Nicci's room?"

"Of course you can. Do you want me to go with you?"

"Yes. I'm not going alone." As April and I tip-toed through the house, we were looked for the intruders causing the disturbances. By this time I needed a cigarette and was too chicken to go outside alone. I asked April to go out on the deck with me while I smoked. *Hopefully being outside would help calm us down.* We could not hear anymore chaos from inside the house, so we deemed it safe to re-enter. As I led the way toward Nicci's room, with April following on my heels, I heard a thumping sound on the wall. Looking up, I saw a white flip-flop sandal fall to the floor beside April.

April screamed. "Oh, my *gawd*, now they are throwing shoes at my head!" She ran past me and vaulted into Nicci's room. Nicci was now awake from April's yelling. April jumped into bed with Nicci. "Can I sleep you with sister?"

"Sure, but shut up and go to sleep. I don't want to know what the yelling was about, or I won't be able to sleep either."

My house was again suddenly silent, but my mind was buzzing with questions. *Why were black human-like shadows standing over my children at night? Why was so much attention being paid to my daughters all of the sudden?* As I sat in the silence of my dark living room my rational mind searched for the answers. I was like a detective piecing together clues. The ETs were showing up at the house again, the increase in strange activity…then it hit me, the season had changed, and autumn was in full swing which meant abduction was imminent…so why had April been singled out? Was it a warning?

13

Contemplations

Why do most of Stan's abductions occur between August and December? There has to be a reason.

My mind never shuts up for very long. A mental vacation for myself, quiet time to let my mind and body rest, time to meditate... these things were a luxury rarely allowed to me, or by me. Even in my sleep I was trying to make sense of the unimaginable, the unbelievable.

Originally, I thought the timing of Stan's abductions had something to do with moon phases but no consistency could be found to support my theory. Stan's first abduction had occurred in September 2001 when three strange looking beings came knocking at Stan's door. As strange as it sounds, that is exactly what happened. That was when Stan met the female extraterrestrial he calls the Possum Lady. The abduction communications between Stan and the Possum Lady revealed many amazing future events, as well as strange pictures, and equations and other information that Stan shares in his book *Answers*. She told him that the extraterrestrials who are in contact with Stan originate from Orion.

Is that a hint or something? I wondered.

I began to ask questions of anyone and everyone I could think to seek out for an answer. No one that I contacted could give me one, nor did they take me seriously when I asked it. And so began hours of research and on-line inquiry yielding little or no information to either support or oppose my notion. The lack of any information suggests to me that no one has seriously posed this question before. So, the following is my own personal thoughts and opinions of what is going on. There are many aspects that I've considered. For starters, The Orion system is the most prominent winter constellation in the night sky. Orion's belt is the most easily identifiable, and has been given many different names throughout the millennia: Our Lady's Wand, the Magi, The Three Kings, or simply the Three Stars. Of this system, the Belt is of the most interest to me, containing the stars, Alnitak, Alnilam, and Mintaka. The Possum Lady said they were located six light years behind Alnitak, in the Orion system, 1360 light years from earth, where they have a good view of the Horsehead nebula. The Zeta Reticuli system is located at a distance of about 39 light years, but can't be seen with the naked eye. Taurus, which hosts the Pleiades (Seven Sisters), is 440 light years from Earth.

These and other systems are said, by Government whistle-blowers as well as other abductees, to be home to many different races of extraterrestrials. *So, how is it possible for these beings to travel so far, so fast?* I asked myself. We have all been taught that the shortest distance between point A and point B is a straight line. But, if you bend the line, as Stan's night writings seem to show, you can traverse the distance very quickly, much like stepping through a doorway. In the second regression with Leo Sprinkle, this symbol was questioned, trying to come to an understanding of what it meant.

Leo Sprinkle (LS): The symbols on the equations that look like pathways, can you describe the meaning of those symbols?

Stan Romanek (SR): They are…connection…they are… mmm…they are bringing two points together. Humans have a hard time…thinking…in a…four-dimensional reality, let alone five or six-dimensional reality.

LS: Those are many dimensions involved in these equations?

SR: There are many ways to travel. You do not need to take years to travel great distances. You can…shorten the distance (gesturing with thumb and forefinger).

LS: Are there doorways or pathways in which space-time is diminished, or…

SR: There are occasions…that make it easier to get from one place to another…you might call them…*(word…)* gates.

LS: Gates?

SR: Gates.

LS: Do you have information about doorways to other parts of space, like wormholes...gates?

SR: Yes. Yes, and so do some humans. They are...we are trying to...push humans in that direction. Humans have been taught incorrectly. There is a more efficient way of travel. They say that...human scientists say that the fastest way from one point to another is a straight line. That is incorrect. You can touch...touch...*(gesturing) bring them together.*

LS: Different parts of space, of the space-time continuum—can bring them together?

SR: 'Continuum'...Space. Bending...space. There are different ways of travel. There are...some that can... by though, there are some that you...can manipulate. There are chemical, spiritual, some you call spiritual, a combination.

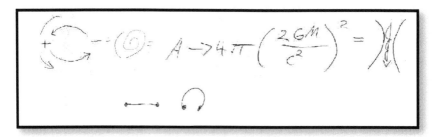

During the 5th regression, this information came out, prompting more questions.

Heidi*:* Why is it easier to make phone contact certain times of the year versus others?

SR*:* It is a matter of...alignment. Humans would not understand. It is matter of alignment, great distances it is hard to communicate.

Heidi*:* Does it have to do with the appearance of the Orion Constellation?

SR*:* More than that but...close. Very good!

The existence of a gateway in the center of the Orion system was revealed many years later during Stan's sixth regression, conducted by Dr. Leo Sprinkle.

SR: It...started on January 11th of 1992. The gate was activated...a gate...a gate...overlap...an Orion gate... center Orion...Alnitak, Alnilam and Mintaka center gate...center star... Alnilam overlap...overlap.... the Orion gate...11-11 gate. That is why Starseed sees 11-11. He is...a major part of that higher density raising...*(mumbling)* higher density, higher density... raising vibrational awareness. The 11-11 gate has been activated...Egypt. It was activated in Egypt.

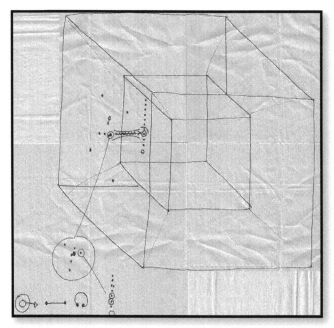

Copyright © 2003 Stan Romanek. All Rights Reserved.

This drawing made by Stan on October 20, 2003 is, I believe, of the Orion stargate. It shows how the Orion beings travel from Orion to Earth. This drawing is of the doorway (stargate) between third density (the inner cube) to the fourth density (the outer cube).

Is there more to Stan's drawings, and the information from the Orions during the regressions, than we are seeing?

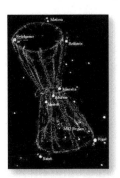
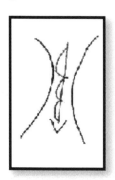
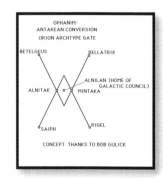

Left to right: Golden Mean, courtesy GoldenMean.info; Drawing by Stan Romanek; Antarean Conversion Orion Archtype Gate, concept thanks to Bob Gulick.

The alignment of Earth and Orion's stargate happens in the fall and winter months. Perhaps this gateway is used by other ETs civilizations as well. I found this picture which resembles the pictures of the Orion system, Stan's drawing of how the ETs get to Earth, and Bob Gulick's concept of the Gateway in Orion being the home of the Galactic council and shows that it extends to the Pleiades and Sirius as well.

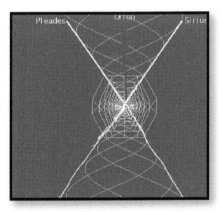

Courtesy GoldenMean.info

Many famous abductees have also experienced this fall/winter abduction pattern. Betty and Barney Hill were abducted September 19, 1961. The Pascagoula Abduction involving Charles Hickson and Calvin Parker was October 11, 1973. Travis Walton's abduction took place November 5, 1975. November 30, 1989 was the Brooklyn Bridge Abduction. The Allagash Abductions, August 26, 1976. On October 16, 1957 Antonio Villas Boas, from Brazil, was taken, and on December 3, 1967, Herbert Schirmer was abducted in Ashland, Nebraska.

The following chart was created by David Wisbey. David was educated at the University of Nebraska, Omaha and Northern

Virginia Community College. David is a professional at creating and editing geospatial data (road networks), geocoding, software testing/debugging. Using reports submitted to the National UFO Reporting Center (NUFORC) showing monthly UFO sightings from 1995 to 2007 lends backing to my theory. In looking at this chart, it shows the months August through December as being increasingly active. The archives at Peter Davenport's website, NUFORC.org, dates back to the 1960s. Upon quick review of the posted UFO sightings since 2007: October 31, 2008 had 1,281 UFO sightings reported; August 5, 2009 had 1,006 sightings; December 12, 2009 had 1,630 sightings; and on November 21, 2010 a whopping 1,367 sightings occurred.

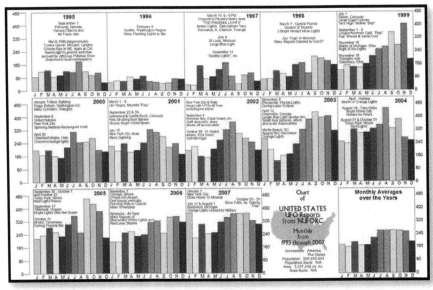

United States UFO Reports from NUFORC — Monthly from 1995 through 2007. Courtesy David Wisbey.

Many people will disagree and doubt my theory, which is perfectly okay. These are my personal thoughts from what I have witnessed with my husband's abductions, as well as many firsthand UFO sightings of my own. But as long as it gets people thinking about the possibilities, as long as it engages people in dialogue, that's all I care about.

Doubting the presence of alien life on earth and other worlds is no longer an option for me. I personally have come to accept the reality of this truth. I don't sit around worrying about if the Orions, the Zetas (Greys), or even the Mantis creatures are real. I know they are. My apprehension is about what will transpire next, who will be involved, and when it will happen.

14

Opening the Door

As I sat on our deck enjoying a beautiful mid-August morning, my mind drifted away. Relishing the feel of the sun warming my skin, I closed my eyes as a warm gentle breeze caressed my bare arms. The sound of my sigh mingled with the chirping of the nearby birds. I had escaped. My moments of solace, though scarce and fleeting, had the power of rejuvenation. Focusing on the sweet sounds of nature around me, the sound of my own breathing and the warmth of the sun felt heavenly. *Don't think about it, Lisa. Just relax and enjoy this moment.*

Then Nicole's angry plea of the night before echoed through my head. The events then came flooding back to mind. The much needed moment of peace was lost.

"Mom, wake up," Nicole whispered at my bedside, shaking my arm. "Stan is outside, again. Tell him to stop knocking on my window!" Turning around she stomped angrily back to her bedroom. *Damn it, will I ever get a full night of sleep?*

Stan's abductions had become so frequent that my response was as second nature as reaching over to turn off the alarm clock. Angrily, I flung the blankets back and launched myself out of bed.

Stop complaining, Lisa. You aren't the one outside, scared out of your wits. Rushing toward the living room, I heard loud knocking at the kitchen door and ran to open it. *What will his story be this time?* I groused. Startled, I stepped back from the door.

"Lisa, let me in." he begged. My frustration quickly turned to panic. A dark, ominous figure draped in black materialized before my eyes. A voice popped into my head.

A vampire can't enter your house unless he's invited....

You watch too many horror movies, I answered back.

The voice spoke again. *Don't open the door...once it's opened, it can't be shut.*

Even though I knew Stan was waiting to be let into the house, the nagging voice of my subconscious was trying to tell me that this was the point of no return. *Snap out of it, Lisa. Stop being such a chicken-shit.*

"Lisa, open the door!" he pleaded as his cold hands jiggled the door handle. Shaking off the feeling of dread, I reached out and released the deadbolt. The click of the lock echoed eerily through my kitchen. My fight-or-flight instinct told me to duck and run, but I knew running wouldn't save me. Stan pushed into the kitchen, the barbeque grill cover wrapped around his shoulders like a cape.

The absurdity of the past few minutes hit me, and laughter bubbled out. This time, however, it was not about Stan's goofy attire; instead I laughed at my own silliness and fear that a vampire might be at my door.

"Are you okay, Stan?"

He didn't answer. At first I thought he was mad at me for not opening the door right away, or maybe for once again laughing.

"Stan, are you okay," I asked again as I followed his quick dash toward the bedroom. *Something strange is going on,* I thought.

Why isn't he freaking out? Why isn't he terrified? Tossing the grill cover on the bedroom floor and kicking it into the corner Stan quickly put clothes on. *Why is he getting dressed, instead of just putting pajama pants on? What the hell is going on?*

"Stan!" I snapped. "Are you okay?"

"Yes, I'm okay. But, Lisa, I need you to come with me. I need to show you something."

"Come with you where?" I asked nervously.

"You have to come outside, into the field, where I woke up."

"Stan, I can't go out there."

"You have to!" he said.

"I don't *have* to do anything." Suddenly feeling the need for self-preservation, I threw up my wall of protection—anger. "Just tell me what happened, and let's get this over with. I want to go back to sleep. There is nothing out in the field that I need to see tonight. It can wait until morning."

"You ... can't wait."

What the hell does that mean? 'You can't wait?' The way he had emphasized 'you' made my heart sink. *What does any of this have to do with me?*

Seething with anger, I followed Stan to the kitchen door. It was then that I noticed the grill cover lying on the deck.

"What the hell is going on?" I said. "The gill cover is on the bedroom floor." I ran back to the bedroom with Stan following hot on my heels. It was gone. "I don't understand. How did it get outside? It was right there a minute ago," I said pointing to the corner where Stan had kicked it.

We once again returned to the deck, picked up the grill cover, and headed toward the field. *Are the ETs testing me? To see how much*

I could take before losing my patience, or my mind? They are still here. I could feel them. Waiting and watching. Why?

"Lisa, I don't want you to freak out, but Nicci was with me in the field."

"What? Why would Nicci be in the field?"

"I don't know why. But she was."

"Show me!" I shouted. My anger was so intense that, in that moment, Stan knew to stay as far out of my reach as possible. It wasn't so much that I blamed him for my children's involvement, I was furious that the aliens had once again abducted one of my babies. *You better hide, you little ET bastards.* Stan directed me to the area in the open space behind the house. There in the church yard, under the light pole, were two definite impressions where a small body and a large body had laid side by side both in the fetal position.

"I need to check on Nicci," I said, running to the house. At full speed I flung open the kitchen door and tore across the living room down the stairs to Nicole's room. When I approached her bed, I found her sound asleep. I noticed grass in her hair, on her bed, and on the floor. *Why did the ETs take Nicci? What did they do to her? She is only 16 years old.*

"Is she okay?" Stan whispered, finally catching up to me.

"*Shhhhh*, she's sleeping."

"Look, Lisa. There is grass everywhere...."

"What are you guys doing in my room?" Nicci suddenly asked, groggy.

"Do you remember anything weird happening tonight? Did you have any strange dreams?" Stan questioned.

181

"No, why?" she asked. I sat on the edge of her bed, and brushed the hair away from her face with my fingers. Grass tumbled out of her long locks.

"Stan thinks that you were out in the field with him," I said as I rubbed her back to hopefully keep her calm. "Did you go outside, when he woke you up to let him in the house?"

"No. I came and got you, Mom. Stan's crazy. I wasn't outside."

"Really, Nicci? Then how did you get grass in your hair and everywhere else?" Stan snapped.

"You probably came down here and put grass in my bed to make it look like I had been outside with you," she answered defensively. At that point, Stan walked out of the room, peeved.

"Don't worry about it Nicci, go back to sleep. I just wanted to make sure you were okay. I'm sorry Stan scared you, banging on your window."

"I'm okay. Goodnight Mommy, I love you."

"I love you too, Nic."

I was prepared for Nicci's denial of the situation but not her anger. It is amazing what we teach our kids without even knowing we are doing it. I had developed a nasty habit of burying all of my negative emotions behind the outward appearance of anger. Fear, sadness, loneliness, and grief all appeared as anger. It seemed Nicci had learned this unfortunate lesson: if all else fails, get mad.

The next morning, Nicci had no recall of the conversation in her bedroom. Her memory was only of Stan waking her up and a feeling of her entire body vibrating like a tuning fork. Both she and April were determined not to believe anything regarding UFOs and aliens. The lesson I had learned after Jake's abduction couldn't be ignored. With Jake, he wanted to talk about the *burglars* that had come into his room, and I wouldn't listen. I told him it was a dream.

With the girls, they didn't want to talk about it, and as luck would have it, I really wanted to listen. There was no way in either of the girls' minds that aliens were visiting their house, or their stepdad. So, how could I talk to them about the possibility that aliens were also visiting them? Was this the door that shouldn't be opened?

As I remained in thought out on the deck, re-living the previous night's events, the sunlight no longer warmed me. I rubbed the chills from my arms as yet another unwanted memory seeped in. *This isn't the first time one or both of my girls have possibly been abducted.* A year earlier, while living in Colorado Springs, April and Nicci had a shared dream. Sharing dreams for my twin daughters was as normal as sharing a bedroom. This one, however, was during a sleepover they had with the girl that lived next door. At 3:00 a.m. screaming from the family room had startled me from my sleep. Rushing down the stairs, I found Nicci shaking and screaming in fear.

"What happened, Honey?" I asked pulling her into my embrace.

"I had a dream that we were on the neighbor's deck, and an alien grabbed me. I was screaming at them to let me go. Stan and April were there too. They said, 'Take her, too, we already have him.' They were pointing at Stan. I don't know what happened to April, I couldn't see her any more. She was gone."

As Nicole related her dream to me, I heard gasps coming from the couch. April was having a full blown panic attack. April lay gasping on the couch unable to draw breath into her lungs. Her legs and arms were flailing as if to ward of an attacker. Efforts to restrain or calm her only increased her struggles. Her heart raced, as tears ran down her face.

"Calm down, Honey. Take deep breaths. Stop struggling, I'm right here," I said. Nicci was pressed against my side, still crying, as the neighbor girl huddled crying in total terror in the corner of the family room. Unable to focus on her, I turned my attention back to Nicci. "Nicci, listen, I know you're scared, but you have to help me calm April down, okay?"

"Apers," she said, "it's me, Nicci...I'm okay and you're okay...we're at home, and mommy is here."

Finally, April's breathing slowed and she stopped fighting.

"No!" April screamed suddenly. I pulled her to a sitting position, and hugged her tight.

"It's all right, you're safe. What happened that scared you so much?" I asked.

"I had a nightmare, that aliens took Stan and Nicci. Mom, it felt so real," she sobbed. It was then, as I listened to April's story, that I realized that the girls had shared a nightmare.

The girls needed me to tell them it was only a nightmare. I needed to be honest with them, that it might not have been a bad dream. How do you calm one fear, only to instill a greater one? I did the only thing I knew to do. I let them believe whatever made them feel safe.

***

The memory of that nightmare made me question whether the girls were also being abducted. I couldn't protect them. I couldn't stop the aliens from doing whatever they wanted to do. And that left me feeling helpless and angry.

What have I done to deserve this punishment? What had my family done to be involved with such horrid things? Why was I chosen to be the one who had to bolt the doors against all monsters, as well as be the one to always open them? I am a prisoner trapped in my own life. How many sleepless nights do I have to endure before I can say my sentence has been served? How many 3:00 a.m. wake up calls do I have to tolerate, only to play mommy to my husband, as well as my children? Why me? Why my children? Why Stan?

"What are you doing, Baby?" Stan asked as he joined me on the deck.

Startled out of my daydream, I jumped in response. "I'm just thinking about last night. Stan, I need you to promise me that won't try to talk to Nicci about this. She isn't ready to accept that she was probably abducted last night. When she is ready, she will ask. I need you to promise me."

"Okay, I promise. But she needs to know."

"I agree, but not until she is ready to hear it. She'll let us know. And so will April," I said.

It wasn't until the spring of 2011 that Nicci finally asked. The mock-up of Stan's second book, *The Orion Regressions,* had just been delivered to the house. She demanded a copy. She already had a copy of *Messages,* Stan's first book about his abductions, but had not yet read it. With both books in hand, she began to read. Nicci's journey to discovering her involvement and her past experiences was literally in her hands. She had made her choice. She had opened the door.

I have gotten to the point of declaring: shit happens, so what? There is nothing I can do except to wait and be ready to help my family deal with the trauma that comes with the visits, and the chaos that they cruelly leave behind. But what happened in the months that followed would leave us reeling, and find us in the emergency room seeking help and searching for more answers.

15

Alien Presents

"This is stupid, why can't Stan stop worrying about UFO stuff? We wanna go *home*," the kids yelled. "Mom, make him get in the van. We hate this. We just want to go home."

Stan had pulled the van to the side of the road, jumped out of the driver's seat and was now standing in a field next to the road.

It was March 26, 2006. We were traveling on I-76 from Nebraska back home to Colorado. Stan noticed what appeared to be a UFO. He always looked up at the sky, especially while driving. His frighteningly unsafe habit made the kids, and me, afraid and angry. We could never get away from the influence these ETs and UFOs had on Stan. Or the way they continually invaded our everyday lives.

The kids continued to yell and whine. They were getting mad at me, too, for not making him stop. I couldn't control Stan's behavior. It was a constant source of arguments between us. His response to our frustrations was telling us, "You're over it," or, "Get over it." And, sadly, he expected us to sit quietly and get over our anger at being inconvenienced by this UFO crap. The kids were fuming. Stan's lack of understanding or acknowledgment of our feelings was very hurtful.

"Stan, get back in the van. We need to get home. I'll watch out the window, and if I see the UFO again I will take pictures," I said, trying to compromise, trying to solve the problem. Stan finally climbed into the van and began driving. When the object again appeared, as I knew it would, Stan tried again to pull over to the side of the road.

"Stan, I said I would take pictures. Please just drive. We are all ready to get home and we are sick of stopping every time you think you may have seen something in the sky."

"I want to get it on video," he insisted. "And if you and your kids don't like it, tough shit. Get over it!"

That was all the abuse I could take for this trip. The UFO temporarily forgotten, I let loose my temper.

"Listen, Stan," I said, trying to remain calm, "I said I would take pictures for you, and all I ask of you is that you not stop anymore. Since apparently everything in our lives has to be about anger, fear, and UFOs, you need to understand that we can't 'Get over it!' You seem to think that the world revolves around you. I have news for you, buddy. It doesn't. Now stop being a selfish bastard and drive the damn van!"

Stan slammed the van in drive again and muttered a few profanities under his breath. Silence fell over the van, not because there was nothing left to say, but because we were all furious. It was best to remain quiet. I was taking pictures out the window as we drove, holding up my end of the agreement. Here is one of the pictures that I took that afternoon. I must say, it is an awesome picture.

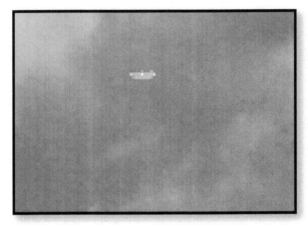

UFO seen from NE I-76. Photo by Lisa Romanek.

A few months later, while painting the house, Stan fell off the ladder and badly injured his right leg. Surgery was scheduled for five days later, to repair the anterior cruciate ligament (ACL) and hamstring. The night before surgery proved to be exhausting. Stan's tossing, turning, moaning, and whining lasted well into the night. At times, his antics were humorous. At other times they were irritating as hell.

"Lisa, do I have to go tomorrow?"

"Yes, Stan, you have to go tomorrow," I said in my sweetest Mommy voice. "Your doctor has already explained this to you. If you don't go for the surgery, you may be a cripple for the rest of your life."

"Do you think I will die?" he asked.

"For *gawd* sake, Stan, of course you're not going to die." I was feeling more like his mommy, at that point, than his wife. "Now, shut up and go to sleep." *Good Lord, Stan is the fourth child I never had, nor wanted.*

"Can we say a prayer?" he asked, on the verge of tears.

"Of course," I said, reaching out to Stan.

He held tightly to my hand as he began to pray. "Dear God, you said where two or more are gathered, it will be. Well, there are two of us gathered, and we ask for your protection tomorrow. Watch over the doctor and guide his hands, keep me safe from harm during this surgery. Thank you for the many blessings you have brought into our lives and for your continued diligence in watching over our family. In Jesus' name we pray, amen."

"Amen," I echoed. "Now, go to sleep, everything will be fine. You'll see."

I'm not sure when Stan finally fell asleep, but his even breathing assured me that he was at least relaxed enough to allow the Sandman to make his rounds for the night. *God will watch over us all* was my last thought before drifting off.

"What's wrong Stan?" I asked into the darkness of our bedroom. "Stan?" *It's so dark in here. What the hell is going on?* Something woke me up. *Was it a scream? Did something fall? Why can't I think clearly?* Reaching across the queen size bed to touch Stan's shoulder as I often did to ensure he was still there, I found him missing. *He's gone! He's gone? Take deep breaths. Calm down.* I scrambled out of bed, looking wildly around the room. *I hate the friggin' dark. Why do they leave me in darkness?*

"The power must be out again. Oh, hell," I whispered.

I went to the attached master bathroom and flipped on the light switch. No power. I began my search, feeling my way through the dark, kicking my feet to search the floor, patting the walls and shower. Back in the bedroom, I continued the same process. Reaching for the light switch, I flipped it on, praying for illumination. Nothing. As I entered the hall, I closed the bedroom door behind me.

Four, five, six steps.

On the right, the hall bathroom. I felt around and flipped on the switch. *Dumbass. The power is out, that's not going to work.* Walking left, the office. *He's outside. Let him in, he's outside.* As if guided by someone else, I fumbled to the kitchen door, unlocked the deadbolt, stepped out onto the deck and yelled Stan's name. No answer. *Flashlight, a flashlight, what the hell is wrong with my brain? Why didn't I think of that sooner?* Leaving the kitchen door wide open, I sidled to the kitchen drawer under the phone and felt around until my fingers found one.

I ran back to the deck, searching the darkness, shining the light across the deck and down into the yard. No sign of Stan. I went back into the house. I had already searched the top floor in darkness. *What should I do now?...breaker box! Get to the breaker box.* I headed to the front door, unlocked it, and stepped out onto the porch. *Get the keys first.* Dashing back up the steps, I snagged the keys from the hook beside the phone and headed again onto the open porch that leads to the garage. For some reason the act of flipping on most of the switches in the house had comforted me, even if there was no power.

Mustering all of my courage, I flung open the front door and ran to the garage. I felt as if I was being watched. As if the aliens were once again observing what I was doing. Entering the garage spooked me, as much as leaving the safety of the house had. I had never been in the garage without lights before. Finally locating the breaker box and positioning the flashlight to shine in the general direction of the panel, I began flipping switches one way and then the other. The garage lights flashed on for a second and then were off again. *What's the problem?*

I began chuckling at myself. "Okay, Lisa, let's try this again," I said out loud. "Flip the breakers one way to turn them on. Flipping back turns them off again. Whew, I think my brain fog is lifting a little." Finally I had some of the breakers on. I rushed back to the house. As I opened the door to step inside, Nicci was standing at the top of the stairs, tears running down her face.

"I thought I was blind," she said between sniffles. "I couldn't see anything."

"You're not blind, Honey," I giggled. Pulling her into my arms I hugged her and rubbed her back. "Go back to bed now, I have to find Stan. He's missing."

"I just saw him standing in the living room," she said. "He went to your bedroom to find you."

"Okay, Honey, go back to bed. I'll see you in the morning. If you need to light a jar candle in your room, go ahead." Stan appeared at the top of the stairs, looking down at me, as if I was guilty of something bad.

"Where have you been?" he snarled at me.

"I was turning on the breakers. Where have *you* been?" I asked, already knowing the likely answer. Stan was oblivious to the fact that he had just returned from being abducted. There were times when I really struggled not to laugh outright, and other times when I just couldn't stop myself, and yet there were times when I just wanted to pop him in the nose. At that moment? I was finding Stan's furious stance...amusing. "Can you go to the garage and make sure all of the breakers are on?" I asked him. If he was going to act like an ass, I would treat him like one.

As he came down the steps and stormed his way past me into the garage, I stood observing him. Already the routine had begun: observe, document, and calm him down. The rest of the lights came on. I ran to the kitchen, shut and relocked the door, turned off the lights, and waited for Stan on the landing. There was something weird going on. I couldn't figure out what it was. I was so sleepy, and all I wanted to do was to go to bed.

Stan came towards me, still unaware that his only attire was his *tighty-whities*. As shocking as the sight of him was, I had to keep my mind working in order to get Stan to realize what had just happened to him. As I followed him up the stairs, a giggle escaped my lips.

"What's so funny?" he asked, his anger finally easing. Now he would be able to accept what I was going to do next.

"Nothing...much," I giggled again, "Your underwear is on backwards."

"I must have put them on fast when I woke up. The lights weren't on, and you were gone. Where were you?" he asked.

Wonderful, he still doesn't understand. I wasn't the one missing. It was time to snap him out of it.

"Stan, change your underwear," I ordered. Stan stood looking at me as if I had three heads.

"You're not the boss of me," he said. *Oh, my fourth child is going to be a pain in my ass tonight...lovely!*

"Do it now," I ordered, "Get clean underwear, and go to the bathroom."

Usually the only time I yelled orders at him was if his blood sugar levels dropped into the twenties. At those times, his life was in my hands, and he has to do what I said or he could slip into a coma. But, from that, I had learned that barking orders at Stan got his attention quickly. It also made him mad. But either way, he was listening. He went to the bathroom with his clean undies in hand and shut the door. I knew the second he realized what had happened. One look in the mirror would confirm the truth in his mind. As soon as he removed his underwear, he would see the blood on them as well.

"Oh shit, not again," he yelled. His brain was fighting to ignore that he had been taken, and from the condition of his underwear. At that point, only God and the aliens knew what had happened. When Stan came out of the bathroom, I was already in bed. I told him that I could not focus on what was going on. My thoughts were so fuzzy, I was becoming nauseous. He said he was suffering from the same feelings. As we laid there we started to hear a whirring sound that made us really sleepy. They next thing we knew, it was morning. We don't remember anything after the whirring sound.

At 6:00 a.m. I made coffee and headed out to the deck to smoke. In a matter of minutes I noticed a huge flattened circle in the yard right below the kitchen windows. It hadn't been there when I went out to the deck with the flashlight. I went into the house and told Stan to get the camera and meet me on the deck. That's when I realized what I had missed last night, what had tugged at my mind, even through the fog. *Stan's leg surgery is today, and he isn't going to go.*

"Stan, how does your leg feel this morning?" I asked. Stan, who had been walking around our room gathering clothes, froze in his steps.

He began to do some kind of crazy hopping, wiggling, high-stepping dance, and was yelling, "Oh my God, my leg is fixed!"

As he twisted around inspecting the back and side of his right leg, the bruising was almost completely gone and there was no swelling. There were five puncture marks down the outside of his leg. "It doesn't hurt at all, how *frickin'* amazing is that?!"

"I'm glad we said that prayer last night," I giggled.

"Baby, it wasn't God that abducted me and fixed my leg. *They* fixed it."

Imagine aliens that give presents. Some might believe that God had given Stan a miracle, but who on earth would believe that he had received this amazing gift from *another* world?

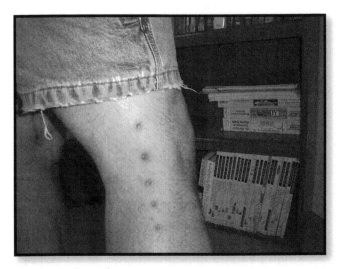

Photo by Lisa Romanek.

Our first course of action was documenting everything. It was then that we realized that Stan's leg brace was missing. I had to leave for work within the hour. I left Stan to search for the missing brace, contact the doctor to cancel his surgery, as well as finish photographing the circle in the back yard.

His surgeon was very angry with him, stating that if he didn't get surgery he would be a cripple. Her assumption was that Stan's fear was driving him to cancel the surgery. He tried reassuring her that he was healed, and wouldn't be a cripple. She instructed him to go to the ER to see her associate who was working that day. He could report to her his findings. Arriving home from work that afternoon, Stan informed me that we had to go to the ER immediately to have his leg checked out. Grabbing the digital tape recorder out of the office, I stuffed it into my sweatshirt pocket, and headed for the hospital. I wasn't going to let an opportunity to record a medical doctor's reaction to Stan's now-healed leg go undocumented. We didn't go so far as telling the doctor that Stan had been abducted, but simply explained what we remembered.

> **Stan:** I woke up at three o'clock. The swelling was gone, the bruising was gone, and everything was gone. And I could run up and down stairs, it was the creepiest thing.
>
> **Doctor:** So if you lose power when you're sick the next time, everything is going to be fine?
>
> **Stan:** I hope so.
>
> **Lisa:** We don't know it's just really odd. We don't know.
>
> **Doctor:** But where did you get the holes? It's a pattern right, I mean, it's right in line.
>
> **Stan:** It was there when I woke up at three o'clock. She woke up because the lights where out I guess.
>
> **Lisa:** And I couldn't...I couldn't find him.
>
> **Doctor:** Do you get up and sleep walk a lot?
>
> **Stan:** No!
>
> **Lisa:** We don't know what's going on either.

Stan: She went out to turn on the lights and then, I was in the living room wondering where she went.

Doctor: Well I don't know what those, you know, those lesions are on your leg or anything, but there's such a pattern, if this, you know, it's hard for me to, to tell if it's from any you know insect or anything like that. More than likely, I don't, could be the, pressure there's no rivets or anything on the knee immobilizer.

Stan: The knee immobilizer is gone, I can't find it anywhere.

Doctor: It just disappeared?

Lisa & Stan: It's gone!

Doctor: You wear it to bed?

Stan: Yes I did! I wore it to bed and it's gone, we looked everywhere for it.

Doctor: Where do you live?

Lisa: Here in [location omitted].

Doctor: Where in [location omitted]? I want to go investigate this. Ah… well… I don't know. But, anyway, the exam is fine today. I wouldn't do anything. Well, I don't know, other than calling Ghostbusters, I think we should just go about our business.

[A nurse entered the room, and the doctor shared his finding with her].

Doctor: Well, he's got ghosts in his house and they stole his knee immobilizer and put holes in his leg. And everything's fine, he's all healed up and now nobody can explain it.

Lisa: Hey, it saved us a hospital bill and surgery!

Doctor: And you know nobody can explain it. His doctor, y'know, was gonna do, it sounds like ACL repair. Now everything is all fine and dandy. You know what I'd do, I would go home, do your normal routine. Big mystery, I don't know.

Lisa: Yea that's what we thought, it's like this is so weird.

Doctor: I still think you ought to call the Ghostbusters.

Stan: I don't think there is a Ghostbusters, or I'd call them.

Lisa: Ghostbusters!

Stan: I don't know what else to do. I was thinking maybe you guys could shed some light on this.

As funny as this exchange sounds, it is word-for-word what was said. The doctor's confusion is evidenced by his babbling. But his seriousness in suggesting we call Ghostbusters amazed me.

I have spent many years being furious with the ETs for abducting my family. I felt justified in my anger, and then suddenly I found myself grateful towards them for healing Stan's knee. Resentment remains for the terror and pandemonium that has ruled our lives, and continues to do so, but my fear of them has unexpectedly eased. In spite of my previous anger and mistrust of the ETs, a new understanding and acceptance crept into my mind. The ETs are not all malevolent, heartless creatures. I can only speak of the ETs that we have been contacted by. There have certainly been a few occasions that the contact was not at all friendly, which complicates things, and points to the possibility that different groups were involved. To clarify, I don't feel that all ETs are benevolent, as I feel the same way about humans.

Over the next few months I struggled with these new emotions. I had a feeling that calling all these extraterrestrial beings "aliens" was not right anymore. The term "alien" now seemed offensive to me, like the "N" word or some other derogatory word. Over time I came to the realization that maybe I could give the ET community a new name, something that was not frightening nor carried a negative connotation: Etherean! Why? Well, ether is the space above the terrestrial plane of Earth, and, according to mythology, the ether was the representation of the upper sky and heaven. I changed the spelling a little to make the word unique. From this point on, I'll refer to the "aliens" as Ethereans, or just ETs.

I only wish I could talk to the Ethereans, and ask them why they fixed Stan's leg. Every day I wish they would talk to me, and answer all of my questions. I have a lot of them. Many times throughout my life I have been told by my mother, "Be careful what you wish for. You just never know when your wish will come true." It is infuriating at times, but...Mom, is always right. Apparently, I am a slow learner.

16

The Uninvited

"I can't…There isn't enough room…Stop…I don't understand …I'll do it, I just don't understand…."

It's 2:35 a.m. Who is Stan arguing with? Searching the darkness of our bedroom, I couldn't see anyone. Stan was sitting on the edge of the bed with his back to me, facing the windows. As he continued to talk to an unseen presence, I listened intently, straining to hear a reply from the dark corner, near where he sat slightly bent over. Then I heard it: a scratching sound—slow and then very fast. I sat up slowly, and began inching my way slowly toward the end of the bed. Stan fell silent. My breathing seemed deafening in the darkness as I gingerly moving forward until I was balancing on my hands and knees. I peeked around Stan's shoulder.

"What does that mean?" he asked. Startled by his sudden outburst, I jumped in response, causing the bed to bounce. "Slow down. I don't understand. I need more room."

Who the hell is he talking to? As I sat there watching him, my eyes finally adjusting to the murkiness of the room, I could see perfectly. Stan was frantically writing another equation.

As Stan continued his conversation with the unseen presence, a bolstering thought zinged into my head causing my heart raced with excitement. *I won't be the only witness. I don't have to go through this alone, again. Don and Heidi are here. I'll go wake up Heidi, so she can see this, too.* In the middle of another recent move, this time into a small apartment, Don and Heidi slept on mattresses in our living room—our fancy guest room.

Heidi and Don came into our lives a year earlier during a presentation about Government disclosure of UFO cover-ups in Denver. Heidi initially approached me, asking if I was Stan's wife. *I do have a name. Why does everyone address me as 'Stan's wife'?* Smiling, in spite of my irritation that no one knew my name, I answered, "Hello, my name is Lisa. Yes, I am Stan's wife."

Her kindness and compassion radiated from her like a living thing, and drew me to her like a bear to honey. As she and I stood talking I learned that she was a mortgage broker. I asked for her business card, and explained that Stan and I were looking to buy a house. She introduced me to her companions, Don and Richard. Don reminded me of rock-n-roll—a teddy bear version of Antonio Banderas, dark and dangerous, yet soft and snuggly. Richard, she explained, was a relator and a professional chef. His deep booming voice laced with a noticeable New Yorker accent made him seem crusty— much like a toasted marshmallow, crisp on the outside and soft and gooey on the inside. Within weeks of our initial meeting, we had all become close friends. Heidi and Richard took on the daunting jobs as our mortgage broker and realtor.

Slowly, so as not to disturb Stan, I eased back into a sitting position on the bed. Swinging my right leg off the bed to the floor, I shifted as much of my weight as possible and stood up without moving the mattress. Stan continued his one-sided conversation with the uninvited visitor as I tip-toed out of the bedroom.

"Heidi, wake up," I whispered patting her leg. "Heidi, Heidi…." It was no use. She wouldn't even stir. Her snores drowned out my whispers. I wondered if Don would wake up. "Don, wake up," I whispered. As soon as I touched his foot, he bolted upright.

"What's wrong? Lisa? Are you okay?" he asked.

"Yeah, I'm okay, come with me," I said quietly. Gesturing with my hand to follow, I led the way into the hall that led to the front door and our bedroom. I could feel Don's presence right behind me. The look on his face was that of confusion and nervousness. "Stan is writing again," I whispered. The confusion instantly cleared from his face. Don and I stood near the end of the bed staring at Stan. We both were afraid to speak for fear of interrupting the writing and communication. I started making hand gestures, a kind of makeshift sign language. Pointing to Don, then to my eye, and then to Stan while moving my hand as if I was writing ("Can you see him writing?") Don would nod affirmatively. Pointing at him, then my ear, and then I wave my hands around the room ("Do you hear anything?") Don shook his head negatively. Don leaned close to my ear, and asked, "What should we do?"

Shrugging my shoulders, I whispered back, "I don't know." Stan suddenly put the paper on the night stand, lay down, and was snoring softly within seconds. Don and I backed out of the room silently.

"That was amazing," Don announced. "Who do you think he was talking to, Lisa?"

"I don't know, but it's pretty creepy." Having unseen and uninvited extraterrestrial visitors prowling around our house at night is something I will never get used to. "Do you want me to sneak in and grab the papers?"

"No," Don replied. "I say we leave everything where it is. Let's wait until morning. That was...very amazing."

"I'm glad you were here. Do you know how much crap I get from people because I am the only witness to these night writings? Apparently, spouses don't make good witnesses."

"What? Why don't spouses make good witnesses?" Don asked.

"I don't know. Some people say ignorant things. Spouses spend at least twelve to eighteen hours a day together, eight of those in the same bed. Significant others are probably the best observers. I have been accused of lying about events in order to make Stan's case look more believable. Hell, I have even been accused of being the 'alien in the window' that we videotaped. But thanks to you, tonight, I have a witness." *I have a witness. No one can call me a liar now.* The full magnitude of what had just happened hit me. Stan was communicating with an alien being, a life form who could communicate without physically being in the same room. What I thought was freaky Don thought was amazing. He was right, not many people can say they talked to an alien. "Okay...well...I'm heading back to bed. See you in the morning, Don. Well, in a couple of hours anyway!"

"Goodnight, Lisa," Don replied.

Sneaking back into the bedroom, I eased back into bed, pulling the blankets up to my ears and snuggled into my pillow. Stan didn't move. His soft, even breathing seemed so odd in contrast with what had just transpired. Getting back to sleep would not come so easily for me. My mind raced with imaginative thoughts about who my goofy husband had been talking to, and why I couldn't hear any voice. *For all I know, he was talking to a flippin' mouse,* I thought. *But if it was a mouse, it was a bossy and confusing one. A mouse that knew about advanced physics equations.* And that is how I spent the next hour. The sound of Don's deep snoring from the living room finally lulled me to sleep.

The next morning, Stan got up and was furious. He was grumbling loudly and venting his anger by slamming drawers. "Damn, kids. They're always making messes for me to clean up."

"Stan, stop slamming stuff around. Everyone is still sleeping."

"Your kids made a mess, again. Why don't you ever make them clean up after themselves?" He was getting madder by the second.

"Stan, the kids didn't make this mess. You did," I snapped.

"Why are you blaming me?" he yelled.

"Stan," I said. "Lower your voice. You wait right there. I'll be right back." I hustled off to the bedroom and got the paper he had written on the night before, slapped it against his chest. "There you go, Stan, figure it out," I said as I ambled to the kitchen to make coffee.

Don and Heidi were now awake. "Morning, Honey. How did you sleep?" Heidi asked as she gave me a hug.

"*Ehhh,*" I said shrugging my shoulders. "As good as any other night, I guess. Stan was writing again last night," I whispered, nodding in his direction.

Stan stood staring at the paper for a long while. Heidi approached him warily, looking over his shoulder to see the paper. I love and appreciate Heidi. She knew how to deal with Stan, and did so gracefully when my anger and frustration prevented me from doing so, or when I just simply didn't want to deal with it. Don and I explained what we had witnessed during the night. Stan just sat there holding the paper, shaking his head in disbelief.

"Who was I talking to? What was I saying? I need a shrink. I think I am losing my mind. I think I've gone bat-shit crazy!" he said. Not knowing exactly what 'bat-shit crazy' meant, I began to laugh. *Being Stan's wife isn't, by any means, easy...but at times, it is entertaining.*

Stan's "poor, pathetic me" victim attitude wore on my last nerve. I wanted to knock some sense into him. If it was legal to beat the crap out of him, to make him see the positives in his life, I would do it on a daily basis. Day in and day out, I am bombarded with his—my fourth child's—freak-outs and break-downs. I no longer tell him that he's not crazy. Instead, I tell him that he is. Why? To shut him up! Sometimes withholding support was another useful defense mechanism—besides anger, it was the only way I could make it through the day.

For whatever reason, I was chosen by the Ethereans to support Stan. *What the hell were they thinking? I have the patience of a gnat, and the temper of a grizzly bear.* Maybe the ETs are trying to teach me a lesson in patience and perseverance. In life, I am a slow learner—

but sometimes it's by choice. Sometimes, I am too stubborn to back down from a fight.

"I'm sick of hearing about you, you, you, Stan. Call a friggin' psychiatrist. And by all means, find someone who will diagnose you as mentally ill. I mean it. If you don't want to be sane, that is your problem. I am done playing the 'poor me' game with you. You are not the only one in this family who has been abducted. You are not the only one who has suffered. You are not—the only one!"

"You are so mean to me," he said.

"Just make some calls."

Stan contacted a counseling psychologist named Dr. Leo Sprinkle. After a short conversation over the phone, Leo agreed to be Stan's regression therapist. Nothing, and I do mean nothing, could have prepared us for what was about to happen.

17

Crazy?

"Lisa, I want to be crazy. If I'm crazy, then none of this is real. I can take a pill and get better. I can be normal again."

What a sissy! I thought. *Why would anyone want to be crazy? For that matter why would anyone want to be normal?* Normal is as much a state of mind as crazy is. Conforming to other people's standards and ideals in order to be considered sane? Normal seems insane.

Dr. Leo Sprinkle, a counseling psychologist and regression therapist, began working with Stan in 2006. As the first regression began, Stan began acting peculiar. His normally calm, relaxed body and voice pattern changed. Stan began referring to himself in the third person, calling himself 'Stan' or 'Starseed'. With eyes closed he began to look around the room, following Clay, Alejandro, and I as if he could see us. Leo looked like a cat that had just been given a warm bowl of cream. His eyes twinkled and a smile spread across his face as he asked, "Do you have a name that Stan and Lisa can call you?"

Wonderful, I thought, *now Leo is addressing Stan in the third person. I think they've both gone whack-a-doodle.*

"My name is not important. What I do is important. But you can call me Grandpa, if you would like."

What? What the hell is going on? Oh crap, Stan is right. He is crazy. Why is he calling himself Grandpa? Stan wanted Leo to tell him he was crazy and give him a magic pill that would make him sane again. *I hope Leo brought the lunatic cure with him.*

"What information is available?" Leo asked.

"You are carving...humans...humans are carving...damage. Human are...creating their own chaos. They are being led to create their own chaos...for gain of evil or...*word*... mmm...money... monetary...mmm, for monetary reasons. And...humans are still very tribal. And...wars...are falsely being...waged...lies...and... over monetary reasons. And this plane is...on the brink of...no return. And we have...chosen to speed up...the learning process. So, there is a chance to possibly correct the damage and the race... can save itself."

Humans? Oh, for goodness sakes, were we being led to believe that Grandpa is an extraterrestrial?! How is this possible? How could a life form from another world be talking to us? I was as fascinated as I was scared. *And to think, six years earlier, I thought the coolest thing that had ever happened to me was meeting Stan, who saw a UFO.*

I was no longer afraid of the ETs that lingered in and around my house at night. Their presence had become familiar. I rather enjoyed their little pranks once I got past my fear. However, I didn't have to talk to them. Now, this ET was calling himself Grandpa. If he thought using a familiar family name would put me at ease, he was incorrect. I had wished for the opportunity to ask the Ethereans questions, but I hadn't really meant it. This fella talking through Stan freaked me the hell out, especially when he spoke directly to me. I wanted him to stop talking to me and to stop looking at me. I could see my husband sitting in the chair, but he was definitely not the man I married.

"*Pssst,*" I whispered to get Leo's attention. I had written a question on a piece of paper, and was trying to hand it to him without disturbing the proceedings.

Grandpa had heard me. Turning his head toward me he scooted quickly to the edge of the chair as if he were about to launch forward. *Oh shit, now I've done it.* Never having been to a party that entertained channeled ETs, I didn't know what to expect. I didn't know what the protocol was. In past regressions, the therapist asked all of the questions, and we acted as observers. I didn't know if the ETs could be violent if provoked unintentionally. I sank back into the couch quickly, fearing that Grandpa was coming after me, thinking that I had angered him, by interrupting him and Leo's conversation. I pressed deeper into the cushions of the sofa. I really thought he was about to pounce on me, like a cat on a mouse.

"You can ask me," Grandpa said smoothly, and relaxed back into his chair.

"Lisa, do you have a question that you want to ask?" Leo chimed in to ease my discomfort. I sat staring at Stan for what seemed like an eternity. I think Grandpa knew he had startled me. Trying to regain my composure and slow my heart rate, I took a few deep breaths. Diverting my gaze to Leo, I shook my head no. Leo sat smiling at me, "It's okay, Lisa. You can ask your question." Flustered and scared, I finally stuttered out my question, or at least part of it, before *he* interrupted me.

"How are your sister, brothers, and your father—?"

"They are in the same genetic line. They are...part of the process to get to Stan. They are...they have been tested, they have been...it has been determined...who is correct, who is right, and who the one to proceed is. It is Stan, it is…his job to…among other things…it is his job to help with the transition."

The full transcripts of all of the communications with Grandpa are in Stan's second book, *The Orion Regressions.*

As much in control as Leo was of the process of the regression, it was very clear who the puppet master was: Grandpa. In *Messages,* Stan tells how the ET's used his vocal chords, but it was much more than that. This being could perceive of us, through Stan. Stan couldn't remember anything that happened during the regressions beyond the first few minutes.

Leo had given Stan just what he had asked for—a magic pill. It was not the kind of pill Stan was seeking, however. Stan was given two options, like in *The Matrix:* the blue pill or the red pill. We have all been given the choice, the choice between blissful ignorance (the blue pill) and embracing the sometimes painful truth of reality (the red pill). What a crazy concept.

In our society, crazy is one of the most widely used words in our language. According to the dictionary, its formal (literal) meanings are: mentally deranged, demented, insane, senseless, impractical, and totally unsound, or not in touch with reality. The informal use of the word crazy is described as intensely enthusiastic, passionately excited. We are 'crazy about baseball'. We 'run like crazy'. We are 'crazy in love'. We get 'stir crazy', how about…'boy/girl crazy'? So, are we all deranged? No! Are we all a tad bit crazy? I sure hope so. Life would be very boring and uneventful if we weren't passionate about life, and all that comes with it.

What was about to happen would serve as a lesson of what happens when you mix the blue pill of ignorance with the red pill of reality. We were soon to learn—reality isn't for sissies.

18

Temper Tantrum

"That's it. I'm done being manipulated by these damn aliens. Who the hell do they think they are?" Stan screamed.

"What are you talking about, Stan?" I asked. "What happened this time?"

"Nothing happened. I just don't want to do this anymore. I am sick of the abductions, the Audrey calls, the regressions, and still not having the answers. I am sick of being told what to do by aliens. Damn it, I want my life back! I want to be normal, like everyone else. I don't want to be the poster child for this weird and bizarre alien crap anymore. I'm done. I am not going to talk to people about it anymore…period. End of story." He continued to yell throughout the house in the hopes that the ETs would also hear his proclamations.

"Do you really think it is that easy?" I asked trying not to lose my own patience. *Here we go again.*

"Oh, yeah, it's that easy. If I don't cooperate and tell my story what can they do about it?"

I began to laugh. *If only it was that easy, I thought. To walk away from all of the weirdness and to have it all just disappear would be a blessing.* We had bought and moved into our new home just two months earlier, our seventh move in seven years, vowing that we would stop running from the aliens and the Black Ops. It was a nice fantasy to think we could truly walk away from all of the strangeness, but I knew we would never escape. *They* wouldn't allow it.

"What do you mean, 'what can they do about it'?" I giggled. "Are you serious, Stan? You have to remember that you are not in the driver's seat in this situation. They are. They'll abduct you again just to show you who's boss."

And that's when the fun started. Stan's temper tantrum had instantly set off an explosion of activity. The ETs had heard him loud and clear. Heidi and I were on the phone, my having just updated her on Stan's angry fit. Stan had headed to bed, and had just shut the bedroom door when I heard the chaos start. The sound of running feet began, traveling back and forth across the roof. I started to laugh, and shared with Heidi what was happening.

"I hope you fall off the roof and break your damn legs!" Stan screamed. "Nothing you do will change my mind. I am finished with all of this crap. Go away and leave me alone." Jake, too, had heard the noises and came running to me for safety.

"It's okay, Jake. This racket has nothing to do with us. The aliens are trying to prove a point to Stan." Jake and I sat on the couch listening to Stan's angry tirade. We were laughing so hard we were crying as Stan continued his one-sided yelling match with the ghostly Ethereans—extraterrestrials on the roof. They responded with loud crashes and pounding feet. It sounded as if my house was being ripped apart by a wrecking ball as the loud thumps and knocks boomed on all sides. Stan was at his wit's end, determined not to back down from the decision he had made. He flung open the bedroom door and ran down the steps to the living room. He saw Jake sitting next to me, the two of us were still laughing uncontrollably.

"Come on Jake, let's go outside and see if we can see them little bastards."

"No way, dude. I'm okay right here," Jake laughed. "Are you really going outside in only your underwear?" The torrent of activity subsided late into the night, only to flare up again the next night. When the invitation to go to the cabin for the weekend was offered, Stan jumped at the chance to get away from home and the ETs. His only condition to going was that none of our friends, who would be joining us, could talk about the ETs, or anything remotely connected to them. Everyone agreed to Stan's terms.

I had accepted that my role in Stan's life went beyond being his wife. I, too, had been given a duty by the Ethereans, and I had spent every day of the past seven years living up to that responsibility—supporting and encouraging Stan while keeping him grounded by deflating his ego when it got too big for his britches. Sometimes, I had to be an outright bitch to accomplish my task. My constantly crooning to him that everything would be okay, and coddling him to make all the bad scary things seem not so frightening, was not going to happen this time. This time, the results of his temper tantrum would be his to deal with, alone. Stan says I am passive-aggressive, but I prefer the term, "aggressively passive."

The ETs would have to deal with Stan in their own way. And what better place for them to teach Stan this lesson than up at the cabin, away from the distraction of civilization? *This will be an interesting weekend,* I thought. *If anything happens, I will personally thwart anyone's attempts to assist Stan.*

19

Search Party

I love the mountains, I thought, breathing in the crisp night mountain air. Richard, Heidi, Don, Clay, Stan and I sat lounging on the deck situated on the south side of the cabin. "Thanks for inviting us for the weekend, Clay. We needed a break," Stan said.

"You're always welcome here," Clay answered. "But I'm surprised you agreed to come up here, Stan. I mean, considering the trouble you've had the past couple of nights, and how safe and secure you feel while you're here...."

Laughter rang out at the unspoken implications in Clay's response. No one mentioned the ETs or Stan's temper tantrum, not directly anyway. In light of Stan's abduction in 2004, while here at the cabin, this was the last place anyone expected Stan to want to spend this particular weekend.

"Shut the hell up," Stan replied, rolling his eyes. He headed to the door to get a refill on his decaffeinated coffee. "Anyone need a beer while I'm going?" Stan asked over his shoulder. Three 'yes, pleases' followed him as he entered the cabin. As soon as Stan was safely out of earshot, I quickly addressed the group.

"Listen, you guys. Stan has made a choice to not cooperate with the extraterrestrials anymore. That is his choice. You all know as well as I do that the past two nights of commotion at our house is not the end of the ETs' harassment of Stan. If, and when, anything happens this weekend, I need you all to ignore it."

"But Lisa, what if he is taken again?" Heidi asked.

"I guess that's the price he has to pay for his stubbornness. *Shhh, Shhh* here he comes."

Everyone probably thought I was being a cold, heartless bitch, but I didn't care. I was fed up with Stan's complaining that he hated the ETs, and then whining that he missed them. It was a lot to handle; I'm still only human. He knew what he was supposed to do, and yet he was refusing to do it. It was time to either put up or shut up.

Returning with the beverages, Stan re-took his seat. The friendly innuendo-laced conversations continued as we relaxed under an azure night sky, devoid of any and all light pollution. The scene above us lent an air of otherworldliness to the darkened forest that wrapped its arms around the cabin, folding us into a cocoon of blackness as shooting stars whizzed occasionally across the sky. The mood was light in spite of Stan's rule of no ET talk.

Suddenly, a high-pitched cry ripped through the forest, echoing off the mountain side. Stan leapt from his chair and plastered himself against the side of the cabin. My warning to him two nights earlier was obviously still on his mind, and his fear that the ETs would show him who was boss surfaced.

Over and over again, we could hear the horrific yipping. "Stop everyone. Stop moving," Heidi yelled in an attempt to be heard over the scrapping sounds of the metal deck chairs as everyone scrambled to their feet. Everyone fell silent. "It's one of the dogs.

One of the dogs is hurt." We had forgotten that Clay and Richard had brought their dogs on this trip, three in total. "*Shhhhh*, everyone be quiet. We have to figure out which direction it's coming from," she ordered.

"Oh, thank *gawd*," Stan said, pushing away from the safety of the cabin wall. "It is just one of the dogs. I thought they were coming to...."

"Don't say it, Stan. We are not allowed to talk about anything related to why you just freaked out. Remember? So deal with it," I snapped.

He glared at me. He was so used to being the center of attention because of the creepy stuff. When no one reacted to his fear with soothing words, he didn't know how to react. And to make matters worse, I threw his own demands back at him, which really ticked him off.

Heidi, Stan, Don, and I retreated to the cabin as Clay and Richard went to retrieve their dogs. The guys entered the cabin a short time later with all three dogs in tow. Clay's dog, Sydney, had a nose and mouth full of porcupine quills. We spent the next hour pulling quills out of her face.

After supper, we cleared the table and set up for a game of cards. Stan eventually went to bed as the rest of us continued to play cards. "Did you see that flash of light?" Richard asked. "It came from the hall, toward your bedroom, where Stan is."

"That's Stan's problem. We are playing cards. Now whose turn is it?" I said as another flash of light erupted in the hall.

"But, don't you think we should check on him?" Heidi asked.

"Hell, no. We aren't going to go check on him. We are here to relax and have fun. Stan demanded that we are to ignore anything concerning the ETs and not discuss it at all. So that's what we are going to do. Whose turn is it?" A few minutes later, Stan came running out of the bedroom, panic written all over his face. "You want to play cards with us again Stan?" I asked.

"Did anyone else see ...?"

"No one saw anything, Stan, nor are we talking about it. Are you playing, or going back to bed?" *Oh this is fun,* I thought. *I can do this all night. Look at all of them bursting at the seams, knowing what Stan had just experienced all alone in the bedroom.* "Is it my turn?" My innocent gaze belied the mischief of my words as I searched the faces of each of my friends. "What? Is something wrong?" I asked innocently. *Fishing in a barrel. This was too easy.* "Play!" I snapped. "Stan, either you join us, go back to bed, or go find something to do."

"Fine, I'm getting in the hot tub. Does anyone want to join me?" he asked. Everyone stood up at once, seeing an opportunity to be away from me so they could ask him questions.

"Sit down," I commanded. Then turning to Stan I said, "We are in the middle of a card game, so I guess you are on your own. Have fun down there all alone, Sweetie," I said.

Ten minutes later, we heard banging on the basement door. Stan bounded immediately to the top of the stairs.

"Did you hear that?" he asked. And the banging started again. Everyone, including me, sprang from their seats. Half of us ran to the deck, the others ran toward the stairs to the basement. We found no one outside the door, nor were the motion sensor lights on.

Stan wouldn't go back to bed until I went with him. I don't know why he thinks my presence in bed will protect him, or why he felt that I would try to stop it, and tonight of all nights! *I'm not getting involved.* But finally, around midnight, I gave in. Scooting Stan toward the bedroom I was too tired to continue to play the part of the holier-than-thou, bitchy wife any longer. *It's just too much damn work.* I thought. *But it sure was fun!* Don followed my lead. He too ambled to his bed located in the loft and surrendered to the sandman's coaxing for slumber.

It turned into a long night. Clay, Richard, and Heidi stayed up until almost 4 a.m. keeping watch to hopefully prevent Stan from being abducted. As everyone moseyed toward their beds, Clay made one last stop. On the loft landing, aiming toward the massive wall of windows on the south side of the cabin, he positioned his video camera to film the entire lower floor, as well as the deck, the driveway, and field. Everyone had finally settled in for what we all hoped would be a quiet night of sleep. Three hours later, I heard Stan banging around the bedroom.

"Lisa, wake up," Stan said.

"I'm already awake. You're about as quiet as a bull in a china shop," I said, flinging my arm over my eyes. "Go away, Stan, I want to sleep."

"Lisa, something happened last night. "

Damn it to hell, why? Why, why, why?! I lifted my arm off of my face and peeked through half-closed eyes. "Oh, my *gawd*, you are such a *dufus*, Stan," I giggled. "Why are you wearing my robe? You look good in pink by the way."

"Yeah, yeah, yeah, laugh all you want. I couldn't find my underwear. I had to put something on."

"Okay, I'm being serious," I said with a straight face. "So, is there something you need to tell me, Stan? Has wearing ladies nightshirts and robes become a weird after-abduction fetish you have developed?"

"Shut up," Stan said, trying not to laugh. He knew I was joking, trying to get him over his panic so he could tell me what happened.

217

"Okay, Stan, so what happened?"

"I had a dream last night, but, now, I don't think it was a dream."

"Why don't you think it was a dream?"

"I'm peeing blood," he said.

"Do you have any marks?" I asked.

"No, I already checked. Can you grab me some underwear out of the suitcase? And my khaki shorts too?" he asked. He sat on the edge of the bed continuing his story as I rummaged thought the suitcase, and tossed him the clothes. "Heidi was with me."

"What do you mean, Heidi was with you?" I asked.

"She followed me down the stairs to the hot tub room in the basement."

"Why were you and Heidi going to the basement?" I asked.

"I don't know. We didn't talk. I just walked down the stairs and Heidi followed me. When we got down the stairs, I noticed the main door was open, and started walking toward it. There was a grey alien standing just outside of the doorway. One of the dogs followed us downstairs, and started growling. The alien pointed a silver pencil-looking thing at the dog, and I felt a strong energy of some kind pass by my leg. The dog started yipping, rolling, running, and crapping all over the basement. Not just a little, it was everywhere!" Stan exclaimed. "That's all I remember."

"Let's check the basement first. If this wasn't a dream, there will still be dog feces all over the floor. I doubt they'd clean up that kind of a mess."

We started down the stairs to the basement, and before we reached the bottom Stan began gagging into his sleeve. It wasn't a dream. There was dog poop everywhere.

"Oh crap, where's Heidi?! We need to check on her too. And the dogs," he said.

We immediately woke up Clay, Richard, and Don. We needed to check on the dogs. Sneaking a peek into Heidi's room, I could see her long red hair splayed out over her pillow and hear her soft snores. At least she was in her bed safe and sound. None of the dogs was wounded but Sydney was acting strange. The poor thing had already had a rough night confronting the backside of a porcupine. Now it appeared she may have had a run in with an extraterrestrial as well.

Clay went to the loft to check the camera. It had been running for three hours but only had one hour of footage on it. He wondered how that was possible as he rewound the tape to the beginning. He watched it in fast forward, hoping to see something approach the camera. It had recorded from 4 a.m., as Clay could see himself on the film walking across the living room on his way to his bedroom. As he got to the end of the tape he only saw himself approach the camera once again to turn it off. There was no way of knowing when the camera was shut off, or when it was restarted, with no sign that anyone else had approached the camera to turn it off. As Stan, Don, and Richard fixed themselves a cup of coffee, they went over the details of the night before. Clay joined them in the kitchen, documenting what time everyone went to bed, if anyone got up to use the bathroom, and what Stan remembered. They then decided to search the field where, two years earlier after Stan was abducted, an eight foot flattened circle had been found.

"Okay, Baby, we are heading out. See you in a bit. Let me know when Heidi wakes up," Stan said. "I want to be here in case she remembers anything,"

"I'll holler at you when breakfast is ready, too," I said.

While Heidi slept I entertained myself with my own thoughts while preparing breakfast. They've formed a search party—a posse. The four rugged city slickers trekking into the remote wilderness of the great Rocky Mountains in search of the 'extraterrestrial' rustlers who had once again invaded the homestead like thieves in the night. Their only goal, retrieve the stolen treasure—Stan's underwear. *At least I have myself to talk to*, I thought. The smell of coffee teased Heidi to awake shortly after the guys had left the cabin.

"Morning, Honey. Where is everyone?" She asked cheerfully.

"They're out in the field. Stan was taken again last night."

"No sir, he was not," she stated simply. She stood in the kitchen with me for a few minutes adding teaspoon after teaspoon of sugar to her cup of coffee, and just a dash of cream. Heidi wandered over to the front windows that overlooked the field to the right of the driveway. A good cup of coffee, in Heidi's view, is brewed with a cup of coffee grounds and eight cups of water. *Turn on the pot and drink it as it brews.* She stared quietly out the window, occasionally nursing a sip of coffee. Usually, she would have had a million questions. Concentration lines formed between her brows.

"Stan wants to talk to you. He asked me to let him know as soon as you got up. Let me yell at the guys and let them know you're awake—that breakfast is almost ready."

"You know, I kind of remember something, but I can't grasp it," she said. "Stan...*hmmm*, we were going to sit in the hot tub. No. *Hmmm....*"

"It's okay, Heidi. You'll remember. Can you watch the eggs for a second? Let me get Stan. It might help if you talk to him."

I went out to the deck and yelled down to the guys that Heidi was awake. When they came into the cabin a few minutes later, Stan was waving something like a banner in the air.

"Well, at least we found my underwear."

"Hurray, the search party was a success," I said triumphantly. Everyone turned and stared at me, having no idea what I was rattling about. I just smiled and continued my silly rendition of a Western saga. "Did ya find evidence that them there ETs had visited the mountain, Pa? " I said smiling, amusing myself. "Sorry, not enough sleep," I said. "Who wants eggs?"

"Actually we did find evidence," Clay said. "We found Stan's underwear on the edge of the field, the side ripped open. There is a twelve-foot flattened circle out in the field with three indentations, about a foot deep and evenly spaced."

"Serve us up some vittles, Ma," Richard chimed in. Stan and Heidi went out on to the deck to talk about the night before. She said that she remembered walking down the stairs behind Stan, as if they were going to go soak in the hot tub. She remembers, like Stan, the Zeta—the grey in the doorway, and Sydney being injured. She didn't have any other memories. Stan filled her in on what he remembered, and that he was sure they had both been abducted. Like clockwork, my mind filled with the usual flood of questions. *Why was Heidi abducted with Stan? Was this part of the reason that she had been placed into our lives? Was she yet another woman from Stan's abductions, like the dark-haired woman?*

In spite of the nagging questions about Heidi and the dark-haired woman, I was feeling on top of the world. My mood was so light that I didn't dwell on the usual negative overtones, such as Stan's infidelity via abduction. I wonder if all spouses think that through abduction their spouses have been unfaithful. I know I have. There are hybrid children to prove that some kind of procreating is happening. And yet, no negative feelings were left behind from this abduction.

Stan and Heidi filled their plates and joined us at the table. Between bites of eggs and bacon, Stan announced, "I know with every fiber of my being what I am supposed to do. I was given the responsibility of being a messenger by the ETs, and that is exactly what I'm going to do. I have to tell my story. I don't have a choice, and they made that very clear. The truth is too important to be ignored."

Just as I had predicted, the Ethereans had taken Stan once again. I can't give you details of what transpired during this abduction, nor can Stan. He has few conscious memories of what happened beyond seeing the alien in the doorway. I would love to be able to weave an enchanted fairytale of how Stan stood before the galactic council and was shown all of the wonders and possibilities that lay at the feet of humanity. I would like to tell you that instead of the ET hand-slapping that I had predicted, Stan was given guidance to fulfill his destiny as a starseed—as a messenger—whose duty it is to guide the world's people to a new understanding: that we are not alone.

However, this isn't a fairytale. It's not a fable filled with the wild ramblings of an insane woman. This is my life. As wild and wacky as it seems, it is real. The moral of the story: a lesson lived is a lesson learned. Sometimes reality has to slap you really, really hard to get your attention before you can accept it. It begged the question: what more loomed in our future because of this lesson?

20

Deepest Darkest Fears Come To Light

"It's you. I remember you," Stan said.

"Hello. My name's Victoria," she replied. "We met at your presentation earlier. And I must say it was amazing." She shifted uncomfortably under Stan's intense stare.

"You look like someone that I met a few years ago," he said. "I don't know how best to say this, so I'm just going to come right out and say it. In a few of my abduction experiences, there was a woman with me on board the ship. You look exactly like her. Actually, I'm almost positive it was you."

After years of desperate searching, Stan had finally found the dark-haired woman from his abduction experiences. Without talking to me first about his epiphany, he had approached her and introduced himself.

"Stan, I believe I've been abducted since I was a child. I have very clear memories of beings, aliens with mitten-like hands in my room as a child. And I have two scoop marks on each of my shins. The scoop on my right leg is very deep. I've always called it my 'alien' scoop. I'm a volunteer for the Extraterrestrial Affairs

Commission in Denver. That's why I came to your presentation today. I was told that if I wanted to see a real case of alien abduction and extraterrestrial contact, this was the place to be."

The Extraterrestrial Affairs Commission was a grassroots effort started in Denver by Jeff Peckman in order to establish an official commission. He had proposed the commission after listening to Stan speak.

"It was nice meeting you, Vicky. My wife is putting on her coat, she must be ready to leave. I'll see you again soon." They exchanged phone numbers and email addresses and promised to stay in contact.

"Please, don't call me Vicky. I hate that name. I was called Vicky as a child, and it doesn't have warm fuzzy memories attached to it. You can either call me Victoria, or V. I'm sure we will talk again very soon."

As I put on my coat, I began scanning the room to find my social butterfly of a husband. Spotting him in a secluded corner of the restaurant talking to a woman I had never met made me uneasy. Who the hell is that, and why the need for privacy? Apparently he was looking for me as well. When our eyes met, he acknowledged me with a wave of his hand. Like a child caught with his hand in the cookie jar, a look of guilt crossed his face, telling me something was amiss. *It's probably nothing to worry about. Stop being jealous. She's probably just another, adoring UFO groupie.* Finishing my goodbyes as I walked towards the front door, Stan was unexpectedly at my side, suddenly in a rush to leave.

"We need to go, we have a long drive home," he said.

"I've been ready. I was waiting for you but you seemed kind of busy over there," I said. We walked to the van in silence, each of us deep in our own thoughts. The drive home was shaping up to be the same.

Stan finally broke the silence with a long litany of statements and questions. "Victoria is such a sweetheart…Victoria is interested in UFOs…Victoria is working with Peckman on the ET Affairs Commission…Did you see the pictures of the bear in Victoria's backyard? Victoria invited us to her house…." Victoria this and Victoria that.

"Who the hell is Victoria?" I finally broke in.

"The woman with the dark hair that I was talking to," he said.

"Okay, that tells me nothing. There were a lot of women with dark hair, and you talked to them all. So which one was Victoria? And why the sudden interest in only her?"

"It's her. I know it is," he said. "I recognized her immediately. When I was getting ready to do my presentation, I saw her walk in and about passed out. It's really her," he exclaimed.

"What the hell are you talking about? Who is 'her'?" I asked.

"She's the woman, the one I was abducted with," he stated. "She speaks Russian but she doesn't have an accent like I remember." As Stan continued to talk about the instant connection he felt with her, my heart squeezed as if in a vise. I fell silent. The shock of his announcement left me stunned, and seething with anger. I felt betrayed; never before had I felt that with Stan, and it consumed me. "What's wrong with you?" he finally asked.

"Nothing!" I snapped. Tears of anger and frustration ran down my cheeks. *This can't be happening. Oh gawd, this can't be happening.* My greatest fear had always been what would happen if or when Stan found the woman from his abductions. Now he had. I sat in silence, staring out the window into the blackness of the night. That was how I felt in that moment, dark and empty. Every time I tried to speak, my throat would tighten, preventing me from venting my anger, my hurt, and my fear. I could feel Stan staring at me across the van but couldn't acknowledge him.

"What the hell is wrong with you?" he yelled. "Why are you acting like this?"

"Why didn't you tell me four hours ago? You've known since before your presentation, and you never mentioned it. Why?" I whispered.

"I didn't want to upset you," he said. My Irish/German temper rose to the surface instantly.

Since when do my feelings matter? "You didn't want to upset me? Are you fucking kidding me? I am beyond upset. I am hurt and I am pissed. Why didn't you introduce me to her at the restaurant? You should have talked to me about this. I am your wife. Why would you just assume that my feelings should be protected, only to tell me about it later? Why did you think that it was a good idea to have this conversation with her, without me? Without telling me what was happening first? Why?"

"I knew you would react like this. That's why. I'm sorry. I should have told you but I didn't want you to freak out and cause a scene," he said. "You would have wanted to go home right away, and I wanted to talk to her more."

"You are a selfish bastard. You are blaming me for this because I would have undoubtedly freaked out. You didn't tell me, so you could talk to her more. Justify it however you want, Stan. Blame your wrong on me if that makes you feel better. But don't you ever hide something of this importance from me again! Do you understand?" No answer came from Stan. Apparently, he couldn't see that what he had done was wrong, or that saying sorry wasn't going to fix everything this time. *"I mean it, Stan. If you ever do something so selfish and so hurtful again, I will leave you."*

My fear and jealously doubled daily as Stan and Victoria's relationship deepened. Daily telephone conversations fed Stan's need to learn everything he could about Victoria. Their conversations took precedence over everything in Stan's life, including me. During a casual conversation, Stan asked, "Victoria, do you have any memories of anything weird happening since childhood?"

"Yes, in mid-March of 2003, something very strange happened," Victoria said. "I remember feeling very alive, like every nerve in my body was turned on and on hyper-drive. I know I was abducted but have few memories of the actual event. This may sound really strange, but for weeks after this experience, I was consumed with the most intense sexual urges," she said.

"Holy shit! Hang on a minute," Stan said. Running to his office, he returned with the original manuscript of his book, *Messages*. He read page 78 of the manuscript to Victoria, where he, too, described how his sexual urges had been overwhelming in mid-March, 2003.

"Stan, this is incredible. Maybe we shared this abduction," Victoria announced.

For whatever reason, I was not aware that Stan had experienced such urges. It really hurt me to read about this in Stan's book, *Messages*, let alone to overhear these conversations from them. *I've become the third wheel in my own marriage.*

Stan and Victoria's endless conversations reminded me of when Stan and I had first met and started dating. Every free minute of every day was spent talking to each other, just like now with Stan and Victoria. The connection, the developing relationship between the two of them made me uncomfortable. Though there wasn't an intimate physical relationship between them, I still felt as if Stan was being unfaithful. My constant fear that eventually they would cross the line of friendship was an ever present fear. I began to envy the time that Stan and Victoria spent together. I would love to have a relationship, a friendship like that with my husband, to feel like I was more than a maid, cook, laundress, and roommate. The ETs did a real number on Stan in 2002. Since that time, he still keeps me at arm's length, insisting that he loves me, can't live without me, and that he couldn't have survived all of this abduction stuff without me, but physically and emotionally he has abandoned me. He has been diagnosed with post-traumatic stress disorder (PTSD) because of his abductions and what was done to him. In return, I struggle to hug him, to tell him I love him, for fear of rejection. It is a vicious cycle of blame, guilt, hurt, loneliness, and rejection that has caused walls in our marriage. I love my husband with every fiber of my being. Someday, I know everything will be okay again. However, Stan didn't have any walls with Victoria, and that terrified me beyond understanding. *Why is their connection to each other so strong, so compelling? Stan and Heidi have a strong friendship as well. Why is Victoria's connection so much more frightening to me?*

Sometimes I think Stan forgets that I am not a simpleton. I have a memory like a steel trap. Once it's in my mind, it doesn't get out. If Victoria was the woman on the space craft with Stan, then the seven children the ETs showed them were theirs. In *Messages*, he shares that, while on the craft, he watched the woman give birth to something. Their eyes met at one point and he didn't see fear in her eyes, he saw despair. Later, in the same abduction, as the two sat side by side naked on a bench, Stan recalls holding her, trying to comfort her, and supporting her weakened body when they were taken into a smaller room. The ETs brought in a group of small children, some barely old enough to walk. That is why Stan and Victoria's connection is so strong, the children. Their children.

I had a feeling there was more going on, that something much larger was at play. I began desperately searching for an answer. In doing research to understand the connections between Stan and Victoria, as well as Stan and Heidi, I came across a hypothesis that purported the ETs could create what is referred to as a "love bite" scenario.

Eve Lorgen is the author of the book, *The Love Bite, Alien Interference in Human Love Relationships.*[1] In it, she shares that the participants feel overwhelming love obsessions for an alien-chosen targeted partner—another abductee. The targeted partner is sometimes another local abductee, and other times the chosen mate is across the country or even in another country. For those abductees who are able to get together, the relationship is often short-lived and passionate, leaving one of the partners in a state of unrequited love. There were many variations to the basic love bite set-up, or manipulated relationship. In most cases the person has numerous alien encounters and/or UFO sightings. In a few cases the targeted love bite partner does not realize him/herself to be an abductee.

As I struggled to understand why the connection was so instantaneous and so strong between Stan and Victoria, I wondered if perhaps they had been "paired" in such a manner. Stan had searched for the woman he remembered from his abductions for five years before finding Victoria.

Lorgen sites a few of the other signs to be memories of bonding scenarios in abductions or vivid dreams. Time and again either

---

[1] Lorgen, Eve Frances. *The Love Bite: Alien Interference in Human Love Relationships.* Bonsall, CA: ELogos & HHC, 1999

partner appears to be in a trance or drugged state. Both individuals are given telepathic messages to initiate contact, either on a verbal level or a more physical, sexual level. If and when the two parties meet in person, as Stan and Victoria did, they have a sense of knowing that meeting this person was not by accident. They feel as if they have known the other person all of their lives, like a soul connection. Paranormal activity also increases during the love bite set-up. Ms. Lorgen explains that she has observed how love bite relationships were set up as a positive perk to an abductee. A non-abductee can be paired with an abductee to help promote the alien agenda without knowing it, with the same feelings of having found your soul mate.

Though I saw these telltale signs in the beginning of their relationship, Stan and Victoria didn't. Maybe it was because I was searching to understand, and they were not. Stan would tell me it was my jealousy and imagination causing me to see what was not there. And I felt his denial was preventing him from seeing the truth that was staring *me* in the face. My jealousy had blinded me in order to see what my research had revealed. I only had to look to understand that Eve had drawn a roadmap. I just had to slow down and read the signs. All roads led right back to Stan and me. Were we matched by the ETs as a means to an end? Was the chaos in our lives simply a staged performance to serve the purpose of enlightening the human race to the reality of ETs? Are the children a manipulation as well?

It took many months to come to grips with Stan and Victoria's friendship. It took much longer for me to establish the deep and loving friendship I now have with Victoria. And though my nagging concerns about infidelity, of Stan leaving me for Victoria, and about the hybrid children are always in the back of my mind, I try to leave them alone and not dwell on it. Though I know Victoria will always be closest to Stan, I have reached a place of peace in my life where the jealous side of me has finally quieted down. At least for the time being.

21

I Quit!

"I love my job. These people are my responsibility, and I take that duty very seriously," I said to my supervisor. "When one of my elderly residents comes to me with a problem, I do my best to try to fix it. Many of the residents are complaining about the new administrator. They don't like her. How do I fix that? If I report her behavior to Human Resources, it will get back to her, and I can't afford to lose my job. "

"I don't know, Lisa," the nurse replied. "I can't do anything about her either. We all know what happened to the last person who complained about the administrator, he ended up fired. I'm like you. I can't risk losing my job either."

Working as a Qualified Medication Administration Personnel (QMAP) in an assisted-living facility brings with it more responsibility than most people realize. These people depend on the staff to help them with almost every aspect of their daily lives. Helping them to get bathed and dressed, comb their hair, read mail that they can no longer see, and so much more. Many residents depended on me and the other girls I work with to be their voices.

I had been caring for these people for three years of my twenty-one year career in health care. They had become like my family.

As soon as they hired the new administrator, it became evident she was not what we were used to. A few of the more outspoken residents had approached her with their concerns and complaints. One such little lady addressed her in the dining room one afternoon. "Excuse me," she said. "Do you realize that you are dressed like a street walker?" Taken aback by the woman's bluntness, the administrator froze in midstride. "People are talking about you," the spunky woman announced. The dining room erupted in laughter. This ninety-eight-pound spitfire said what everyone in that room was thinking but were too afraid to say. Cheers from all corners rang out in support of her claim.

"How I dress is none of your business. And if I wanted your opinion," she said looking around the room, "I would have damn well asked for it. Now sit down and eat your lunch, keep your mouth shut, and your opinions to yourself." The echo of shocked gasps sounded as loud as the cheers had moments earlier. I was furious. *How dare she talk to a resident like that. This is their home, she only works here.*

"I'll be right back," I said to the other QMAP. "This shit is going to stop right here and right now." I marched out of the dining room and up the stairs to my supervisor, the facility nurse. As I explained what had happened, she became as enraged as I was.

"This has gone on long enough. I will make a call to her boss and report her if you think I should," she said.

"I don't expect you to do anything yet," I said. "We are all so afraid of her and of losing our jobs that we will not stand up for what is right. That's not okay. I will not sit by any longer while she treats our residents this way. If I do, I am as guilty as she is, as are all of you. I am not asking you to take a stand. I will do that myself. All I ask is that you back me up, no matter what happens. If I get fired, and she remains in this building, someone had better step up right behind me. I will talk to the other girls so they are aware what I have decided to do."

"Lisa, what exactly are you going to do?" she asked.

"I'm going to write a letter of resignation. I'm tired of worrying about being fired, so I'll quit! It's time to give the big bosses the whole truth about what had been going on in this building. I'll let them know that if they don't do something about her, after getting my letter, I will make sure to take it a step farther. I will call the ombudsman. They will launch an investigation."

I had to get back to work. My decision had been made. Now I had to find the courage to follow through with it. As I re-entered the dining room, the sight of the tall blonde woman wearing a tight black miniskirt, thigh high boots, and a tight, red satin blouse solidified my decision. This woman was indeed dressed like a hooker, not as an administrator of an assisted-living facility. She was like a virus that had infected the building, causing everyone to become ill from stress and fear. I could not stand to be in the same room with her.

I turned in my resignation to the administrator and my supervisor on November 17, 2008 at 7:00 a.m., and went about doing my job the best I could. The two-page letter explained why she should not be running our facility. I gave detailed accounts of how condescending, threatening, and disrespectful she had been to the staff, residents and their families. Going into great detail about the way she dressed, I also wrote that I had to agree with the residents, she did dress like a street walker. Figuring I was going to be fired by 9:00 a.m., I faxed the remaining copy to her boss, the head of human resources, as well as the head of personnel.

My pager went off at 9:00 a.m. Checking the message, it read, "Lisa, call on line three."

I answered the phone, as I always did, "Hello, this is Lisa. How can I help you?"

"Audrey just called," Stan yelled. "She said, 'Tell Lisa not to leave her place of employment, it will be taken care of today.' So, don't turn in your letter."

"Stan, it's too late. I already did. Why didn't Audrey call last night when I was writing the damn thing?" As I hung up the phone my pager went off again. The same message was on the screen. I went back into the kitchen and picked up the receiver, not sure who to expect on the other end. As I greeted the caller, relief washed over me. It was Victoria.

"Hi, Lis. Listen, Audrey just called me, and asked that I call you. She said she called Stan as well, but here is the message: 'Hello, Victoria. I do not think Starseed heard the whole conversation, so please tell Lisa that she should not leave her place of employment. The problem has already been taken care of, and tomorrow will be a better day for her at work.'"

"Unless Audrey can rewind time, it's a little too late. They have already gotten my resignation," I said to Victoria. "Thanks for the call, V. I'll let you know what happens."

I waited patiently for the axe to fall, but it didn't happen. I was becoming very unnerved by the whole situation. Neither the administrator nor the nurse had approached me for any reason. I went about my day totally distracted, looking over my shoulder constantly for signs of reprisal from anyone.

After serving lunch and completing my medication pass, the other girls and I went on our lunch break and out for a quick smoke before we got back to work. I was walking up the hall towards my medication room when I ran into the administrator's boss. I was scared stiff. He stopped and waited for me to approach him. "Hi, how's your day going?" he asked.

"Well, I have had better days," I said with a false smile plastered on my face.

"Sorry to hear that. I hope it gets better," he said patting my shoulder as he walked away.

"Me too," I said. *What the hell is going on here? He knows who I am. I've worked here for three years. Why didn't he say anything about the letter?* As I continued walking down the hall, I met the second person I had faxed my resignation to. *Holy crap, two out of the three are in the building. That is never a good sign. That's why I haven't been talked to yet. They have called in the big wigs to deal with me.* I was in a panic. The fear was apparently evident by the look on my face. A co-worker grabbed my arm and pulled me into the medication room.

"Listen to me, Lisa. You said you were prepared to be fired today if they would only listen to your complaints and do something about them. Now, calm down. It will be okay."

I took a deep breath. She was right. That was what I had said, and I meant it. I took another deep breath, opened the door, and went about doing my job. If they were going to fire me, however, they would have to find me to do it. I was not about to make it easy for them.

One of the ladies I needed to administer eye drops for was in the front lobby by the office. I really didn't want to get that close to the office but I had no choice. I had already spotted the third of the management staff I had faxed the letter to wandering around. As I dashed through the lobby, staying as quiet as possible so as not to draw attention to myself, I heard someone calling my name. Fear paralyzed me for a few seconds, and then I realized that my name had been whispered. *"Psssst,* Lisa," the voice hissed again. "Lisa, come here." As I looked around the couch, I saw one of the personal care providers, kneeling on the floor next to a resident. She waved me over, "Come here," she whispered again. As I approached, she said in an excited soft voice, "They just escorted the administrator from the building."

"What? Are you serious?" I murmured back.

"Yes, I'm serious. They packed all of her office stuff in boxes, sat them outside on the curb, walked her out the door, and told her not to return to the premises."

"Oh, my *gawd*, that is amazing. *Yeahhhhhhh*," I said clapping my hands in my excitement. As I breathed a sigh of relief, the feeling was unbelievable and indescribable. I was so thrilled by the news that she had been removed from the building that I ran excitedly from room to room to find my co-workers to let them know what had happened. Most of them were aware of what was going on in my life with the ETs, and that Audrey had called after I had turned in my letter of resignation. *Holy cow, what had Audrey done to give rise to this? Maybe it was a team effort. Together we made it happen.*

Management called all the staff into a meeting and told us that the administrator would not be coming back, that she had been fired.

Am I next? I asked myself.

"Do not ask questions, as they will not be answered. Do not talk about it amongst yourselves. It is not worth wasting your time with," the head of human resources extolled. "Have a good afternoon, and I will see you in the morning. I will be the acting administrator until a replacement can be found." I began to laugh. I was not getting fired.

Audrey's call would prove right. The next day was as if a weight had been lifted. Everyone was rested from the first good night sleep that any of us had had in over a month. I can't say for sure if it was the doing of Audrey and her group, or even if my letter had anything to do with her being fired, but I like to think that we both had a hand in it. Upper management wouldn't even talk to me about it. The only acknowledgment I got was during my exit interview a week later. "We just want you to know that we received your letter of resignation and appreciated your honesty. Are you sure you want to leave? You can withdrawal your resignation if you want to."

"No, I am happy with the way you all handled the situation, but I am still resigning my position," I said. Nothing more was offered, and when I asked if my letter had played a part in her removal, I was told that it wasn't important. *Those words are eerily familiar*, I thought. I could hear Grandpa's words echoing through Stan's mouth: *It's not important.*

Courage is not the absence of fear. Courage is the willingness to act in spite of your fear. And trust me, I was terrified. My co-workers also learned an important lesson. They learned that I was willing to stand up for them, as well as the people we cared for, at any cost. My only hope is that they understand that I did it out of love and not out of responsibility.

Where did my courage come from? Honestly, my courage came from having already faced many of my greatest fears. Fear of abuse, divorce, losing my children, extraterrestrials, abductions, and death. And, in spite of it all, surviving to tell the tales.

I was soon to learn that the battle I raged against the administrator had more to do with who I was, than what I was making a stand against. It was not just about courage versus fear, or even right versus wrong. It was about me, being me, staying true to what I *felt*.

22

Finding My Own Story

Because of Stan's dyslexia, I started journaling Stan's story, thinking it had to be turned into a book. I devoted every spare moment to writing. In May 2005, while we were still living in Colorado Springs, that all changed. Stan and I got into a huge argument, which began with his simple question, "Lisa, have you put the book on disk yet?"

"Yes, Stan I have it on disk. You helped me do it. Remember?"

"When did you do that?" Stan questioned. "I don't remember helping you."

"Stan, please trust me. It's taken care of, and you need to stop worrying about the book. I am writing it, and I don't have time to reassure you every ten minutes that it is under control. "

Stan bothered me incessantly about working on the book. However, working a full-time job, taking care of a house, being a mom, taking care of Stan's emerging health issue as well his abduction experiences, left little time for me or writing.

"Can I see it?" Stan asked with a look of exaggerated innocence on his face. He knew he was ticking me off, but that's Stan—pushing until he gets his way.

"Fine, if you want to see the damn thing, I'll get it. Then you can shut up and leave me alone about it." I marched up to the bedroom and opened the drawer where I kept the satchel containing the printed manuscript and its back-up disk. I grabbed the disk out of the case and headed downstairs. I froze in mid-step, realizing the stack of two hundred or so pages of my printed manuscript and notes were gone. My confusion turned to panic and then to anger. Running back to my room, I ripped the drawers out of my nightstand, dumping the contents onto the bed and floor. *Where are they?* Like a volcano, my anger erupted. Marching down the stairs in search of my husband, I began screaming. "Stan, where are they?! What did you do with them?" The disappearance of the manuscript and the timing of Stan's questioning made me suspect that he was responsible, that he was playing a trick on me to teach me some lesson.

"What the hell are you talking about?" he yelled back. Accusations and hateful words were carelessly thrown like grenades—the effect: emotional devastation and resentment. As my fury began to dissipate, Stan and I agreed that it must have been stolen, much as the UFO file had been on so many occasions in the past. My final words hung in the air, like an oppressive stench.

"I'm done, I'm not going to finish writing the book. And you can all...go to hell."

The next day I arrived home from work to find a message on the answering machine from none other than Audrey:

"Hello Stan and Lisa. We did not mean to cause an argument. We took it, so they wouldn't. If you check your postal container you will see that it has been returned."

Without hesitation, I marched out to the mailbox and, sure enough, inside was my manuscript. On the back, the words, "Finish It" were burned into it.

"How dare they try to manipulate me like this! I meant what I said!" I yelled into the air, "I will not 'Finish It'!"

Stan wrote *Messages: The World's Most Documented Extraterrestrial Contact Story,* telling his own story of abduction. In 2008, I finished writing my version of the story and found a great editor named Garrison Hardy (pseudonym) to look it over. My friend Lucie had introduced us, and in the months that had followed that introduction, he and I had become close friends.

"It's not good, Lisa," Garrison said after reviewing the manuscript. "Why are you telling Stan's story again?" My heart sunk, I felt proud of what I had accomplished. And being told it wasn't good was a bitter pill to swallow.

"I'm telling my side of the story," I mumbled.

"I beg to differ. This is all about Stan," he said shaking the massive pile of paper towards me. "There is not one shred of you, your feelings, or your understandings in this manuscript. Now, here is what I suggest you do. Rewrite it, and this time, tell your story."

"How do I do that, Garrison? How do I tell my story without telling Stan's?"

"Oh, Lisa," he sighed. "Don't you understand how important you are? There is someone that I want you to meet," he said. "His name is John. He and I go back a long way. I think he could really help you to understand your importance better than I could. Can we meet again tomorrow? I'll call John and request a meeting with him at my house."

Arriving at Garrison's house the next day, I was feeling pretty nervous. *Who is this John?* I wondered. Garrison wouldn't tell me much about him. Other than he was a wise man who could help me uncover my inner-self. "Lisa I'd like to introduce you to John," he said.

"Hello, John, It's nice to meet you," I said as I shook his weathered hand. "I know you from somewhere. Have we met before?" I asked.

"It's nice to meet you as well, Lisa. And to answer your question, yes, we have met before. Our first meeting was at Lucie's house when your husband opened the predictions he had written some years ago. We weren't officially introduced, however, so I wasn't sure you would remember me. My focus that day was solely on your husband, but I remember you as quiet and withdrawn from the proceedings. When Garrison asked that I meet with you and explained the reason, I accepted without your invitation. I usually require the person who needs the meeting to ask for assistance. But in your case, I made an exception," he said with a wink.

"Of course, now I remember, you were sitting in the kitchen, watching over the railing as if it were a balcony seat at the opera. I thought you were cute as a button," I said. He chuckled, and blushed.

"I have been called many things in my many years, but never cute as a button," he said.

"Stan teases me often about my habit of finding cute little elderly people at the store that I want to take home with me—like a kid with a lost puppy."

John's eyes twinkled with mischief. His long, fuzzy white locks dangled along his sun-kissed and weathered face, accentuating his smile, a smile that had probably melted many a heart in his younger days.

"Lisa, I have already explained to John why I asked him here today. What I would like for you to do is to tell him about the book you are going to write."

I launched into my story, sharing the basic details of Stan's abductions, and that I wanted to write a book to help others in my situation.

"Garrison, I see why you asked on Lisa's behalf for this meeting. She can't see past her husband to see herself. She really doesn't know how important she is," John announced.

"I'm not important," I giggled, suddenly feeling self-conscious and embarrassed. "How in the world do you think I'm important?"

"Lisa, you are exasperating, " Garrison grumbled. And so began my first session with John, one of many that spanned the next few weeks. It was a battle that many saints would have run from. Like an exorcism, my negativity and my self-doubt had to be removed, and I had to work hard to do it.

Early one morning, I called John. "Hello John, are you open to meet today? I would like to continue our *Where's Waldo* session," I joked sarcastically.

"That would be lovely. I'm having lunch with Lucie today. We could get together afterwards? "

After lunch, John and I went for coffee at a nearby coffee shop. John and I got right to work.

"Lisa, when you look in the mirror, what do you see?" John asked.

"Me." *That's a silly question, who else would I see in the mirror?*

"And who are you?" John gently prodded.

"Lisa Romanek, Stan's wife. April, Nicci, and Jake's mom," I proudly announced, as if I had actually understood what John was trying to get at.

243

"Lisa, if that is all you see when you look in the mirror, we have a lot of work to do before you can even begin to write a book of the magnitude you wish to write. You are important. You are going to have to really look inside yourself, step out of your husband's shadow, and own your power to see the real you," John coaxed.

Own my power? I pondered his words. *What the hell does 'own your power' mean?* All of my life I was led to believe that I was just Lisa, nothing special, no one important. And now John was telling me otherwise.

"John, I just want to write a book to help spouses of abductees, like me. Maybe some of what I have learned will help them. If there had been a How-to-Cope-with-Your-Spouse-and-Abduction manual written years ago, it would have helped me understand what to expect. I wouldn't have had to struggle to find my own way, all the while thinking I was going crazy. There were so many years that I berated myself for being a bad wife, for feeling angry. And all the while it was a natural response."

"Lisa, who are you? And what is your role in Stan's life?" John asked sternly.

Feeling foolish, I began talking out loud to myself and to John. "I am still confused but let me give this a try. My name is Lisa— only a name. Stan's wife, mate, lover. The kids' mom and caregiver. Power? I have no clue. Lord, this is difficult. How can I figure out the answer if I don't understand the question?"

"Okay, let's try something else. What makes you...you?" John asked, as if hinting at an answer. *This would be easier if you would just tell me what you know, ya crazy little shit,* I thought. Somehow I knew John could see me in a different light than I could see myself, as if by some means he could see into my heart, mind, and spirit. "What is it about you that people like?" he urged.

"Do you mean, what good traits do I possess?" Again, he nodded, and remained silent. Taking a deep breath, I began thinking about what I like about myself, and what others may also like. "I'm a loving person. Understanding, compassionate, forgiving, funny, respectful, loyal, affectionate, giving, empathetic, honest, and protective." John sat smiling at me, as if he had witnessed such a strange display of inane babbling many times. "But I have bad qualities, too," I said. "We all have flaws, no one is perfect. I am argumentative, stubborn, ornery, and grouchy."

"Actually, Lisa, I believe we are all perfect, whole and complete, just the way we are. For this exercise, we will look at what you feel are the good and we will address what you feel are not good later. Tell me, what do those good qualities tell you about yourself?"

"That, I'm nice?" I questioned. *Oh, if he wasn't so darn adorable, I would poke him in the eye.* My frustration was starting to show. John took the lead, finally explaining what I struggled to acknowledge.

"Lisa, that is who you are, all of those qualities define you. The Divine Feminine is your power. There are six qualities of the Divine Feminine," he expounded. "The six include the Goddess, the Priestess, the Lover, the Mother, the Amazon, and the Wise Woman."

What in the world have I gotten myself into? I mused. *Self-awareness...own your power...step out of Stan's shadow...The Divine Feminine...This little fella isn't making any sense.*

"The Goddess shows up as compassionate, welcoming, creative, nonjudgmental, open, heart-centered, spiritually-focused, supportive, inspirational, erotic, and loving. The Priestess is thoughtful, reflective, having depth to her presence and intellect. The Lover is sensual. She is open and invites you to touch—her mind, body, and soul. She relishes connection with others. She appreciates beauty in all its forms. The Mother's demeanor is seasoned and carries wisdom. She is benevolent, evenhanded, calm, strong, caring, present, passionate, and protective. The Amazon/ Warrior-ess qualities are: decisiveness and clarity of thought, selfless service, genuine humility, strength of courage. The Wise Woman has intuitive wisdom which comes forward during crisis and intense need. The Divine Feminine is this unseen dimension of soul to which we are all connected on some level, through our instincts, our feelings, and the longing imagination of the heart." As the hours flew by, I began to understand that love is the root of all goodness, and that I am indeed important.

"Wow, that's amazing," I whispered. What I had initially thought were senile ramblings was making total sense. A realization washed over me. *Every abductee's spouse at one time or another has probably felt as worthless and useless as I had. We become so used to playing second fiddle that we lose sight of the fact that we are, in fact, lead banjo. The love and support we give is the one reason that our spouses can get up every day. We are important to the survival of our spouse's emotional wellbeing.* As a spouse of an abductee, I have felt lost, hidden from view by the drama and trauma of my significant other's abductions. We all have a little hidden power, a connection to the Divine Feminine, or whatever you wish to call it, we just have to find it, and own it.

John continued to explain, "Stan is an abductee. That is his story. Your story is what you have experienced and what you have learned from being the support, the wife, the mother, the caregiver to him and your family. Your family would have collapsed without you. That is your story. You are the glue, the binding that holds the clan together. You can no longer remain in Stan's shadow as the wife of an abductee."

Amazing, I thought. John was a mystery, half-crazy, half-genius, and all sunshine. John, it turns out, is a Wiseman, not just a wise man. There is a huge difference in being wise in life and being wise beyond life, and that pretty much sums up John.

My second meeting with him occurred a week later, and although I still knew very little about him, our friendship had grown. The trust we shared made me feel like a kindred spirit. I had, on many occasions, tried to share my revelations with Stan in regards to my working with John, but Stan was consumed with finding his own answers. He didn't have time to worry about what I was doing.

At the end of our second meeting, I grumbled, "John, I really think you could help Stan. I have been trying to tell him about you, but he just won't listen. He just keeps saying that he needs to talk to some guy named Lazarus. "

"Lisa, I will let you in on a little secret. Stan called me yesterday, and we have scheduled a meeting for the day after tomorrow."

In a state of confusion, I sat staring at him. "*You*...are Lazarus?" I asked.

"Yes, but let's keep it a secret until I meet with Stan, as a lesson for Stan to learn to listen, not only to himself but to you as well. It will be a surprise."

I learned that Stan had given John the nickname "Lazarus" the day of the opening of the predictions. Stan shares these prediction in his book *Answers*.

"Lisa, all you have to remember is to function from the heart, only from the heart in everything you do, and with everyone you meet. Own your power," John said.

As I sat looking at John, I realized that finding my own story was only half of the battle. The real triumph was even greater: finding myself.

23

Life's Little Surprises

"Victoria, I don't care what Audrey said," I snapped, almost dropping the phone.

"Lisa, we have to do what she says, " Victoria insisted. "You know from your own experience with her that she doesn't call unless it's important. And this is important. Audrey said that Stan may be missing for a while, but not to worry. He would be returned safely."

"Why can't you all understand that Audrey is not all powerful? I will no longer allow a voice over the phone to dictate what I do or don't do. Do you remember that Audrey called after my mom was in her car accident and in the intensive care unit? She told me not to travel to Nebraska when my mother's life was hanging in the balance because it wasn't safe, and that they were in a better position to help her than I was. I stopped thinking she was all powerful then. After that phone call, I became so angry that I screamed through the house, 'Audrey, I am only going to say this once, so you had better pay very close attention. I am going to see my mom. If you have the ability to help her then by all means do it.

But you better make sure it's safe for me to travel to Nebraska to be with her, because I am going!' Do you remember that?"

"I understand how you feel, Lisa, but she said—"

"How do we even know if it was the real Audrey?" I interrupted. "What if we're setting Stan up for abduction by the Black Ops? I don't like keeping this a secret from Stan," I sobbed.

Stan's book *Messages* had just been released, and now Audrey was dictating that we have a surprise book release party for him at Victoria's house. And not only to have a party, but to allow room for an extra guest that would arrive to meet Stan. *What kind of insanity is this? Why would Stan have to be missing for a while? If it was the real Audrey, the ET Audrey, they would just freeze time. We wouldn't even know it had happened. Something isn't right with this situation.*

Heidi and Victoria called me repeatedly over the next couple of days trying to convince me to make sure Stan was at his party. I told them I would make sure he was there, one way or another.

"You know better than I what is best for you and Stan," Victoria said. "If you think we should tell him, then by all means tell him. I will leave that up to you."

"Thanks V, I appreciate that. Let me think about it, and I'll talk to you later. Bye." As the day wore on, more tears of frustration overtook me. I needed guidance, I knew I wanted to tell Stan the truth, the whole story, but I didn't want to upset him or my friends by ruining the surprise of his book release party.

The phone began to ring again for what seemed the thirtieth time that day, and I was becoming irritated. "Hello?" I snapped.

"Hi, Lisa. It's John. Can you come over here, please? We need to talk. And don't bring Stan with you. It's important," he said.

"How do you do that, John? I was just thinking about calling you," I said. "Yes, I'll be right over. I need to talk to you about something, too."

When I arrived, I broke down in tears, my emotions finally bursting forth. I was finally able to talk to someone who would actually listen to my concerns, and not throw Audrey in my face. I spilled the whole story. Through sobs, I explained that I wasn't okay with what was being planned.

"I was invited to the party as well. I will not be attending for the exact reasons you are struggling with. I will not be part of setting anyone up to be abducted. That is not how I operate," he said. "What do you plan to do about this situation?"

"I think I will go home and tell Stan the whole truth. He has a right to know that his friends are setting him on the edge of a cliff, and that they are willing to push him off simply because Audrey told them to! He has a right to know what he is walking into and to decide if he is willing to go."

"Good for you, Lisa. I am proud of you."

The conversation with Stan didn't go as well as I had hoped it would.

"Stan, we need to talk," I said. "I need to you come outside, so that what I have to say won't easily be overheard by anyone listening over the phone lines or from any other listening device inside the house."

"What is this about Lisa?" Stan grumbled.

"I don't know how to tell you this, so I'm just going to say it. Victoria is planning a surprise book release party for you on Wednesday." He was angry that I had spoiled the surprise about the party.

"Why would you tell me and ruin the surprise? You don't want me to have anything good happen, do you?!" Stan yelled angrily. "You suck."

As much as it hurt my feelings and made me angry to be talked to in this manner, I was used to it. I knew I had to push forward—to help him understand why. "Stan, there is more to it than just a surprise party," I sniffled. "I wouldn't ruin a surprise for no good reason. So if you can just sit down, stop being pissed and listen, you will understand why I ruined your damn surprise. Audrey called Victoria, Rick, and Heidi telling Victoria to throw you a party. She said that you will be abducted. I have cried for days worrying about this. So I decided to tell you, and allow you to decide if you still want to go or not. If it was me, and something this big was being kept from me, I would want to be told." Stan sat in silence for a few moments, digesting my words, then suddenly erupted.

"Hell no, I don't want to go! Are they crazy? Why wouldn't Heidi, Victoria, or Rick tell me about this?"

"Because Audrey told them not to tell you, and not to let me tell you! And, there's more to it. A special visitor will arrive to meet you. I don't like it. I think we are all being set up by the Black Ops."

"You know what, to hell with it. I'm going. "

"Wait, you're what? "

"I'm going to the party. They went to a lot of work getting it set up, and now that I'm aware of what could happen, I'll make sure it doesn't...."

I was hesitant about keeping this party on schedule. But since the surprise was blown, I had already made plans with Heidi and Victoria to have a second surprise party at my house the following Saturday. On *our* terms. I called Victoria as soon as Stan and I had finished our conversation. "Okay, Victoria, I will get Stan there at 5:00 p.m. But I have one condition: he can't be left alone for even a second. I told him we are meeting at your house, and then going to Rick's Paranormal Research Forum meeting. V, will you call the others on the list of selected guests and let them know? Audrey, if you can hear me, the real party is at my house on Saturday."

"Yep, I will call everyone. Audrey, we hope you can make it to both parties, but especially the one Saturday. Okay, Sweetie, I will see you Wednesday," she said.

Victoria, Heidi, and I had begun talking to Audrey during our normal calls to each other, knowing that if we were being monitored, she would be aware of the plans. I was not willing to live my life being dictated to by a voice on the phone. But, I am not stupid. If Audrey could pull strings like she did at my work, then more power to her. I would give out the information.

The party at Victoria's was a lot of fun. I was glad I had made Stan aware of what was going on. He had a great time, too, trying to shake his friends, the ever present shadows that followed his every move, even to the bathroom. True to their word, Stan was never without an escort.

The sudden arrival of a black helicopter hovering over Victoria's house, though, told me that I had been right. This wasn't a party planned by the ET Audrey. In Stan's book *Answers*, he shares that there is the possibility of three different Audreys, and how this party was a set up by the Black Ops using the Audrey voice as a deception tool. No surprise guest showed up, fortunately, nor did Stan disappear for any amount of time. Our friends didn't know that I had spoiled their surprise, nor that I had warned Stan about a possible abduction. I couldn't convince them to see my side of reason, no matter how I tried, so I had to do what I felt was best for my husband. If they ever learned the truth, I was willing to suffer their wrath later.

Saturday arrived, and I had everything planned for the real party. There was no way Stan would figure out anything was afoot. He would have his surprise party, and Garrison, my editor friend, was bringing Stan an added surprise about the book. Mark was coming up to take Stan to a movie. Stan's sister and I would get the party ready, and then get everyone hidden before their return.

The surprise proved a huge success. When Stan arrived, nothing seemed out of place. I met him and Mark in the kitchen and asked them how the movie was, then wandered out the back door to where all of the guests were hiding. As he and Mark walked onto the deck, Stan was met with a huge, "Surprise!!!" He broke down in tears. Garrison approached to give him his gift.

"Could I have everyone's attention please?" Garrison said. "I have a little gift for you, Stan," he said, rattling the paper he held in his hand for dramatic effect. "Stan, congratulations. Your book, *Messages: The Worlds Most Documented Extraterrestrial Contact Story* just went #1 on Amazon's UFO list! You, my friend, are officially a best-selling author." Stan almost fell over. He was so shocked by the news.

"This is the best day of my life. Thank you all for being here with me to celebrate." Tears streamed down his face as everyone lined up to hug and congratulate him on writing such an amazing book.

The party moved inside as the beautiful spring evening had given way to rain. The party began winding down, and many of the guests began to leave. That's when Stan noticed a small child standing in our driveway. As he watched her, she smiled at him through the window.

"Who lets their little girl stand outside in the freezing rain?" he asked. Someone was talking to him, drawing his attention from the window, and when he looked back a few minutes later, the child was still standing there. He became concerned that she must be cold, and went to the door to ask if she was lost, or needed help. When he opened the front door, she ran away. He relayed his concern to Victoria and a few other guests, but he was ignored.

"She's probably a neighbor's kid, Stan, don't worry about it," V intoned. Later, Stan walked past the kitchen window when movement outside caught his attention.

"Holy crap, she's back," he yelled. "The tiny dark-haired child is standing in the driveway again." He ran to the door again, but she was gone. Shaking his head, he grabbed the camera off the table, and headed for the door. Rick, who is ever observant to Stan's spastic behavior, followed him. Stan and Rick returned a short time later with a picture of the child. The most amazingly angelic child I have ever seen. Stan shares the entire story in *Answers*.

April handed Stan the phone. "Who is it?" Stan asked as it rang again.

"How am I supposed to know? I'm not psychic," she grumbled. The phone rang again.

"Hello?" Stan said, plugging one ear. "Hold on I can't hear you," he said walking down to the family room, away from the excited chatted of the throng of guests. Alejandro and I followed him. "Yes, I can hear you...I Love you, too...Hello?...Hello?" Stan collapsed in the hallway. Sobs wracked his body as he struggled to regain his footing. He staggered to the office, trying to hide his tears.

"What's wrong Stan? Who was on the phone?" I asked.

"It was...my daughter." My heart sunk. When he finally gained his composure he explained, "I thought it was my daughter, my real daughter at first. But it didn't make sense, she sounded different. It was the girl from the picture. *She is my daughter."*

"What did she say, Stan?"

"She said, 'Daddy, can you hear me? I love you. Don't worry. I am all right.'" After relating the phone conversation to everyone, the party wound down and the remaining guests finally left. Stan and I headed to bed. It had been an exhausting day, but a day none of us will ever forget.

A few days after the party, Stan began secluding himself in his office. *Something is wrong,* I thought. *Stan is acting weird.* He had been on the phone with Victoria for nearly an hour, and then he had called Heidi and Rick. Though I wasn't aware of the conversations, I could tell Stan was scared. Of what I had no idea.

"Stan, what's wrong? Are you still concerned about the little girl in the picture? Is something going on that I need to know about?"

"No."

"You are acting so weird. What's with all the closed door conversations with everyone?" I asked.

"Nothing, don't worry about it," he snapped.

Don't worry about it? Once again, I was to be the last person to know what was happening in my own life.

"So, you can talk to everyone else about what is bothering you, but you can't talk to me? That sucks Stan. Why am I at the bottom of your list?" With that, I walked out of the room. He was keeping me in the dark, again. Three days passed with Stan became increasingly closed off. He came out of his office to use the restroom, eat his meals, and then he ran back into his office, closing the door, closing me out. He came to bed, long after he knew I was asleep.

My anxiety grew with each passing day. Something was horribly wrong.

As I approached Stan's office, ready to demand an answer once and for all, I heard him say over the phone, "I need you to call Lisa, and tell her."

Tell me what? I wondered. My imagination ran wild. *Who is he talking to and what do they need to tell to me?*

"I can't," he said. "I just can't do it. She is going to be very upset. You have to do it. I know what I said, but someone has to tell her, now." I opened the door, and stood glaring at him. The terror in his eyes told me that he knew he had just been busted. He became very flustered. "I have to go," he said, slamming the phone into its cradle.

"What in the hell is going on Stan? I am tired of being ignored and told nothing. Who was on the phone?" I demanded. "You had better start talking or I'm leaving. I'm sick of being left out of things that affect my life."

"It was Victoria. She said she will call you later."

"Why?"

"I don't know. She just wants to talk to you."

"You are a liar!" I screamed. "I heard you telling her she had to call me and tell me something. Now what is this about?" Stan continued to sit at his desk, staring me in the face, refusing to tell me what the big secret of the past few days was. I walked away, heading to the deck, my mind abuzz with fear. All of the jealousy that I had covered up was now clawing its way out of where I had buried it. *He's leaving me for Victoria and he can't tell me. Why would he make her tell me?* Stan appeared in the doorway with the phone in his hand.

"It's for you," he said handing me the phone.

257

"Who is it?" I asked angrily.

"It's Victoria. She needs to talk to you," he said.

My fear was so overwhelming that I sat staring at him, unwilling or unable to reach out to take the phone. He put the phone on the patio table and walked away, returning once again to the safety of his office. I sat for what seemed like forever, looking at the phone. Finally I reached out and picked it up. "Hello, V," I said, my voice shaking.

"Hi, Lisa. There is something that I have to tell you. But first I need you to understand that I wanted to tell you days ago, but Stan refused to let me. I am very angry at him for putting me in this position. For making me tell you after he said he would take care of it, and didn't. I think you have a right to know what has happened."'

"Okay, so what's he forcing you to tell me?" I asked.

"I got a call from a little girl. I was in my car heading home from the airport. The call came from a 303 number, so I didn't record it," she explained. "Up until now, all the Audrey calls were coming from either 000-000-0000, or unknown number, or from our own home or cell numbers. Honestly I was too stunned to do anything, including drive. The little girl told me, 'Mommy, I love you. Don't worry, I'm fine. Don't be sad, someday we'll see each other again.' Stan didn't want you to know about it because he thought you would be upset. You're not upset are you?"

It was official. Stan and Victoria and the children were a family. And what's worse is that I was left in the dark about it all. No one wanted to reach out to tell me. It was all forced. *What else is Stan not telling me, out of his own stupid cowardice?*

"I am more than upset right now, V, I am furious. Why didn't you call me and tell me this right away? I thought you and I were friends as much as you and Stan are. Why am I the last person to know about something so important? Why does Stan think he can hide this kind of information from me when it affects my life as well? That stupid son of a bitch! I warned him not to ever do this to me again! Did you know this isn't the first time that *he* decided not to tell me something that was very devastating to me? Do you know when the first time he betrayed my trust was, Victoria? The day he met you!"

"Why does everything about his relationship with you have to be such a damn secret? I was scared to death, thinking he was going to leave me for you! The past three days have been a nightmare of worries. His behavior over the past year has caused me a lot of heartache. His need to keep you all to himself, to keep secrets from me, and to flaunt your status as the 'mother of the hybrid children' in my face, has caused me a lot of pain. He doesn't care if my feelings are hurt. He doesn't care if I am upset. And the really sad part of this whole mess is I feel that most of the time he does this intentionally to upset me. And you didn't tell me either."

"Lisa, please calm down. I'm sorry that I didn't tell you right away. And I'm sorry that you are angry. Stan didn't want any of us to tell you, to protect you from being hurt."

"What did you say? Who else knows about this that didn't have the courtesy as my friend to call me and talk to me?" I snapped.

"Heidi and Rick also know, but Stan wouldn't let them tell you either."

"Wouldn't let them? Are you fucking kidding me? Did he threaten to kill you all if you told me? Anything short of that wouldn't have stopped me from calling any of you with this kind of information. I get it now. The great Starseed spoke and his little followers wouldn't cross him for fear of *what*? Let me guess. Being banned from his group? No longer his friends? Honest to *gawd*, what is wrong with all of you?"

"I know, it was wrong, and we all argued with Stan that this was getting worse by the day. The longer he kept it from you, the worse it was going to be. I swear, Lisa, it will never happen again. I am so sorry. Please don't be mad at me. I was forced to keep quiet and then forced to tell you because Stan realized that he had made a huge mistake, and didn't know how to get himself out of the mess he had created."

"I am very upset right now, V, but I will call you later. Right now I need to deal with my husband. Okay. I'll talk to you later. Bye."

I lit a cigarette, and sat swinging on my glider swing trying to calm my emotions. Tears still ran down my face as I struggled to decide what to do next. I knew my options: pack my suitcases and leave, or stay and continue to fight. Most women would say, 'This is a no-brainer. Pack and run.' I, however, am not most women. The most ridiculous part of this whole situation was that I would have been able to deal with the kid calling Victoria had Stan just talked to me. I would have felt hurt, but that was my problem, not theirs. The call itself wasn't why I was angry. Stan had betrayed me once again, as had all of my friends.

I had spent the past year coming to terms with the mystery woman from Stan's abductions: Victoria. Now they were forcing me to deal with the hybrid children—their hybrid children—invading my life. All I could assume is that I wasn't allowed to be a part of the joy they all were sharing, because I wasn't a parent of the children, that I may be upset by the news that they are real. God forbid that I might be upset and ruin all of their happiness about these children. I felt no joy in the knowledge that the children were now coming forward. That the child who had called Stan "Daddy" was the little girl who called Victoria "Mommy"—how could I find happiness in that? I had been lied to by my friends and my husband. How could I trust any of them again? The only emotion I had about the hybrid kids from that moment on was anger.

Stan chose that moment to check on me. Like a bird searching for a make-believe worm, he wandered onto the deck, acting as if nothing was wrong. He just stood in front of me, gazing at the ground. My anger boiled over. "You are a fucking coward!" I said through gritted teeth.

"I'm sorry, I know I was wrong not to tell you," he said.

"You're sorry? Is that all you have to say to me. Do you think 'Sorry' is going to fix this? Sorry?" I said, shaking my head. "How dare you keep this from me. And why would you put Victoria in the position of cleaning up the mess you created? It really hurts me that you can't talk to me about the things that are really important, not only to you and Victoria, but to me, too. This affects me as well."

"I know. I said I was sorry."

"You also promised me after the last time you did this to me that it would never happen again. I can understand your forgetting to share the Audrey calls with me, they happen so often now. But this? This is different. The kids may be yours and V's, but I am your wife. Not Victoria. Not Heidi. And yet they were both first made aware of it, as was Rick. Why did you insist they not tell me? Why?!" I sobbed.

"I knew you would be upset by this news. So I wanted to figure out a way to tell you."

"Stan, the call was made three days ago. You couldn't figure out a way to tell me in three days? And then took the chicken-shit way out by making V tell me anyway? I told you after the incident in Colorado Springs when you met Victoria, if you ever did this to me again, I would leave you. Now I have to decide what to do next."

I had recently been in Stan's position, and had also waited three days to talk to him about what I had been keeping a secret from him—his surprise party that I felt was an abduction set up. Only I was the one who was told not to tell Stan. I can't even justify why it took me three days to do what I knew was right. But I had, in the end, told him everything. My anger overruled my common sense, and I lashed out at Stan.

"Are you kidding me?" he replied. "You would leave me for something as stupid as this? You are psychotic. It's not that big of a deal." Stan knew what buttons to push to piss me off on a good day. And this…was not a good day. His words cut me to the core. I had every right to be angry, every right to be hurt by his disloyalty. My anger fired anew. I stomped into the house, marched up the stairs to our bedroom, and began packing. As I began throwing underwear, socks, shoes, and clothes out of the closet onto a huge pile in the middle of the bedroom floor, I could barely see through the tears.

Stan walked in shortly after, "What are you doing?" he asked.

"I am packing your shit. You can call your sister to come get you, but I want you out of my house today!" I screamed. "You can't even see that what you did to me was wrong, can you?" Stan walked out of the bedroom, slamming the door behind him. I collapsed to the floor, sobbing my heart out. That's where I remained until I couldn't cry any more. I was numb. Blissfully numb. And that is how Stan found me an hour later—in a spent pile on the bedroom floor.

As I lay on the floor hating the world, hating my friends, and hating my husband for their betrayal, John's words echoed in my mind. *Own your power, and function from the heart. Your power is the Divine Feminine: humility, understanding, compassion, honesty, grace, forgiveness, and unconditional love.* Calm settled over me. *This too shall pass*, I thought. I got up, and moved forward.

I didn't run away, and Stan refused leave. On one hand, I understood why he felt he had to protect me from being hurt by this news. On the other hand, I couldn't get him to understand that his not telling me had hurt me worse. I forgave him, and my friends. That's what you do when you love someone, you forgive them.

The maternal side of me couldn't ignore Stan and Victoria's feelings of love for this tiny being. She was their child, and that brought them joy. My belief is that this child is the result of rape of the mother and father by the ETs. That is how I felt. However, she is still a living, breathing child who doesn't deserve condemnation from anyone, regardless of her unusual half-human, half-Orion genetics. The abductions had brought all of us together, for a purpose. Our cosmic connection revealed itself with the appearance of this little hybrid girl. That is not Victoria or Stan's fault. So, putting my hurt and anger aside, I called Victoria to apologize.

"Hello, Victoria. Are you okay?" I asked when she answered the phone, sobs from the other end of the phone line being my only greeting. "Listen V, I'm sorry I said those things to you. I was angry at Stan and all of you for not telling me. I shouldn't have taken it out on you like that. It was wrong of me to be so cruel."

"I understand, Lisa," she said still sobbing. "But you really hurt me with the things you said. If that is how you feel, I will stay out of your life."

"V, listen, I am going to be honest with you. We should have had this conversation a long time ago, and without anger involved. The way you feel right now is how I have been feeling for a long time. Alienation, anger, sadness, and hurt are emotions I have been feeling every day since Stan first found you. Negative emotions have been eating at me, and I have allowed myself to become a prisoner to my own fear. I can't help the way I feel, but you shouldn't make me feel guilty for feeling them. I have been put in the position of defending my place in Stan's life as his wife, while you step in and function as his partner and forget your place as his friend. After this moment on, V, there will be boundaries in place, and I will not allow them to be crossed. I am Stan's wife. You are our friend, and I expect the same respect I give to all of you to be given to me in return. Do you understand?"

"Yes, and I'm sorry. I had no idea I had hurt you so much," Victoria responded. "I now understand it hasn't been easy for you to accept me and my role in your lives as I thought it was. I love you, Lisa, thank you for allowing me to be part of your lives." Our conversation ended with heartfelt, honest I love you's.

I have had people over the years ask me why I stay with my husband through all of these terrifying events and heartaches. My answer is now, and always will be, because I love him.

My justification may seem strange, but I look at it this way: If Stan had cancer, would people ask me why I stay? No, they wouldn't. And that is how I have to look at this. It is much the same situation. Abductions are like cancer, eating away at the victim. No one gets to decide when or if it happens to them. No one can wish it away. And you sure as hell can't run from it, nor abandon the people you love in spite of it! Abductees feel like victims. Many always will. The shame, fear, anger, and other negative effects are an abductee's form of cancer. Once those are purged, we become abduction survivors.

Holy hell, I thought, *I'm beginning to sound like John. Own your power, free your fears, and function only from the heart.* As the old saying goes, with age comes wisdom, and John had both. So, I listened to the wily old coot when he spoke. I am now forty-two and getting wiser by the day. His wisdom has, indeed, rubbed off on me. What I now know is that our involvement, our connection with the extraterrestrials, whoever they are, is bigger than me, bigger than Stan, traversing beyond my household and many friends, extending to millions of people in every corner of the earth…and beyond the stars.

24

My Children, Your Children, Our Children

"Humans are a conglomeration. Humans are mainly a conglomeration of Orion and something else...Sirian. There are other things mixed in. There are multiple races. There will be an extra race to help with the Ascension...what you call 'The Shift.'"

The regression of March 7, 2010 was well underway. A new consciousness came through Stan. This being's purpose was to share a new understanding with Stan, John, Leo, and me.

"Are you yourself Orion that is speaking through Stan?" asked Leo.

"No. I am what you call...*Ehlo...Ehlo..Heem*

"Elohim?" John asked. The look of excitement that crossed John's face told me that something big had just happened.

John and Stan had been meeting for months, much as John and I had been, but for much different reasons. While I was on a journey of self-discovery, and self-empowerment, Stan sought understanding. He had, on many occasions, felt as though some of the ETs he was encountering were different.

During one encounter, a grey ET stood beside our bed. He said, "This is how we allow you to see us," and he waved his hands around his body. "It is because this is familiar, most humans are aware of this form." Stan was unafraid as the being continued to talk to him. "Most humans cannot conceive of our true form, or our true origin, they have not yet been prepared." Suddenly, the five foot tall grey being ran his hand along the side of his body, literally unzipping his skin. Stan was nearly blinded by the seven foot blue light that emanated from the small little grey. "Do not fear us. This is how we really appear. We will come again. You will understand when you are ready to know the truth." As Stan shares in *Answers,* they did come again. And what they shared with him was confusing. They called themselves Elohim.

John is very aware of the angelic realm, to say the least. He couldn't believe that the Elohim were back on Earth, and he couldn't easily explain why they were masquerading as ETs, let alone communicating with a chosen abductee. The confusion surrounding these two encounters is why this regression was executed.

John later explained to me that Elohim, to most people, means God. There has been some confusion throughout religious history that Elohim refers to a singular being, instead of a group of beings. Some refer to the Elohim as the Trinity or Trine. Trinity encompasses the Father, Son and Holy Spirit, three aspects of Elohim—God. How does this confusion happen, you may ask. Because man has flaws, one flaw being their inability to convey correct information. Much like the childhood game Telephone, where a person whispers something to the person next to him, the message continues down the line until it finally ends up back to the person who began the message. Rarely is the relayed message the same as the original. The human mind hears what it is told and tries to figure out what the message behind the words is, thereby changing the chosen words and consequently changing its meaning altogether. "Elohim" is like the word "family." The word itself is singular, but inside the singular are brothers, sister, aunts, uncles, and cousins. So Elohim becomes a divine family, its members many.

Seeing an opportunity to ask for information regarding the hybrid children, I scribbled notes on a piece of paper and passed it to John.

"What can you tell us about these hybrid girls? Why are they here?" John questioned, impatiently batting at a white lock of hair that had fallen across his wizened eyes. His long winged brows arched in pleasure. There was no hiding that he was finding great pleasure speaking to this particular being.

"They are to help with…the transition. To help. They are able to traverse third and fourth densities. They are of Stan. Stan is of Orion. Stan is of human. They are of Stan and the ones around him. There are nine and they are a part of him," the Elohim explained. Leo and I had talked before the session. So he was quite aware of my need for answers regarding the kids. This was not Grandpa, this particular consciousness speaking through Stan was much higher. So Leo hadn't addressed my concerns. But John's question had been answered. *The Elohim know of the hybrid children.*

"Can you tell us what Lisa's role is with the nine hybrids that have been revealed?" Leo prodded.

"She is with Starseed. She supports Starseed. One of the nine is from…part of Lisa and part of Starseed as…a test, scientific test… experiment."

"Like research?" Leo asked.

"Yes, research," he said. "We wanted to create a... multidimensional being. Do you understand?"

"I do," John replied. *That makes one of us,* I thought. *Since when did I become an experiment?*

"Of the nine, one is most important. She calls herself Kioma. There are three in succession. First is Kioma, Trilly is third. The other one has no name yet." [He holds up Stan's right hand and "counts" by holding up both his index finger and his middle finger.]

"Does that mean she just names herself?" Leo asked.

"Yes. That is correct," he replied.

"What is Heidi's role then?" Leo asked.

"Heidi is one of the nine [meaning mother of one of the nine children], Lisa is one of the nine. And there are seven more of the other [Victoria being the other]. The children have called," he said.

One of the calls he was referring to was an introduction by the children. Stan and Heidi were having a conversation one afternoon, when their call was interrupted by a small voice.

"Daddy don't worry we're fine. It's too dangerous for us there right now. You couldn't protect us even if you wanted to. We didn't mean to interrupt your call, but we thought you should know, there are nine of us. Seven of the same, and two, each one with different. I am the oldest. I am named Kioma. It means Trinity. And Heidi..."

"Yes?" Heidi replied.

"For you, my sister's name is Trilly. It means to shine."

Now that these hybrid children had names attached, it was hard to remain indifferent to them. But I did. The children tried to call to speak to me, on a few occasions, but I wouldn't allow myself to become emotionally involved with the kids. Knowing they existed and were reaching out to their mothers was hard enough. I was still struggling to accept that they were real—that the children were becoming a very real part of our lives.

Already I was being forced not only to understand these other women's roles in my husband's life. But now, I was expected to only have positive emotions where the hybrids were concerned. Stan, Heidi, and Victoria practically demanded it because they could feel no other emotion but love, joy, and excitement. I couldn't do that. I was always made to feel that my feelings were wrong. As usual, I was looking at the bigger picture, they weren't. They were so ecstatic that these children existed, and to them that was all that mattered. They are a part of something amazing. They are mothers of hybrid children and that makes them feel special.

"Can you tell us how Victoria came to be a part of the hybrid creation?"

"She was pre-chosen just like Starseed was pre-chosen. It is just, genetics…genetics. Heidi and Lisa…later they were associated. They were…*mmm*…it was a test." The fact that she had been pre-chosen was validation for Victoria that her contact during childhood with the ETs was connected to what she later would become a part of—her connection to Stan was for creating seven hybrid children.

"Do all of the hybrids have blue eyes?

"Orion's are not genetically born with blue eyes. They must become enlightened to obtain the blue eyes. Kioma and the children, there are some that do not have blue eyes. But, from Lisa…Lisa… Lisa's child is very smart," he said. We learned during a previous regression that of the nine children, six are girls and three are boys.

"Which one is Lisa's child?"

"Lisa's child, unnamed. She, Kioma and Trilly...they are friends...sisters...they play a major role."

Sisters? Until that moment, I hadn't considered that the hybrid children were related. However, the truth is that they are. Stan is the father, Victoria, Heidi and I—the mothers.

We are not the only three women in the world who are struggling to understand. There are many women, as well as men, who have been abducted who wonder if they too have hybrid children. The anger and frustration I feel stems from knowing they exist, but that we cannot see them, hold them, and care for them. We worry that they will not know a mother's love as they should.

Leo began to question the Elohim about how many other races, besides the Orion's and Greys/Zetas, were creating hybrid children. "Are there other hybrid races that are also going to be a part of the earth other than the Orions?"

"Yes. There are some that are here now. There are multiple. This is not just for the human race, this is for multiple races. There is a connection. There is a, oneness. "

"Part of the information that we have been given says that one of the races, just as you stated, will be helped by hybrids who will literally bring the vibrations to their own world through the DNA of the hybrids. Is that accurate?" Leo asked.

"They [the hybrid children] will also be helped in other ways," the Elohim replied. "But, yes. There is...we hope that this will affect multiple races at multiple levels. Greys...weak DNA...they have forgotten about spirituality. There are multiple levels of races that are...advanced more mentally. And they have forgotten their place and their genetic makeup have become weak because of this. It is a... for the human race it must be a combining...a melding of the two, technological and spiritual...to make a much stronger human race.

This is where Starseed comes in, by enlightening humanity…that there is more outside of their own world. It will happen naturally. The shift will happen naturally. Stan is here to help…mmm…ease the transition. He is here to…help the transition. He is here to help others to understand that there is more. That's all it takes. It is very simple, but it is a daunting task. "

The Elohim said it so effortlessly: A very simple but daunting task! That is an understatement of a lifetime—of our lifetime. It hasn't been simple. We have been discouraged at every turn. We have been intimidated by Black Ops, as well as by our own fear. Though ten years, nearly eleven now, may not seem like a lifetime to many people, to Stan and I it does. We were thrown into an existence not of our making. We were given a life of strange and frightening events, ideas, and responsibilities. Our lives have been battered and bruised by abductions, ripped to shreds by the betrayal of friends, sullied by anger, polluted by criticism. And my children and friends have suffered the pain right along with us. Walls of sadness and resentment were placed between Stan and me. Our marriage, our love for each other, has been tested and proved. So what has been accomplished in light of all of the chaos that we have endured in this lifetime? Enlightenment? Understanding? Acceptance? Absolutely!

Today is someday. The someday that I have been waiting for. And finally it's all okay.

My daughter, Nicci, is now married. She stood up and exchanged the vows of, "for better or for worse, for richer or poorer, in sickness and in health." She will soon understand the struggles of us, her parents, and eventually what being a mom is all about. Oh, the glory that lies at her feet. She will stumble on that glory, but she too will understand life's lessons, in time.

Jake is questioning God. He is seventeen and coming of age in a world of hate and anger, hunger and oppression, fear and death. I mean who doesn't eventually question His existence? Jake's confusion is that people believe in a spirit not of Earth, God, an extraterrestrial in his own right, but they do not accept the possibility of life beyond Earth. I see where his confusions come from. He will in time understand, and share his knowledge with his children.

April's journey has begun. After a four-month sojourn to Nebraska to find peace and quiet, to get away from the paranormal weirdness that has been a part of her life for the past ten years, suddenly she has awakened. She is now feeling the energies of different places as well as people. She, like many people around the world, is experiencing something amazing. A knowing. Knowledge of things she has never studied or questioned suddenly fills her mind. Quantum reality? Trust me when I tell you this small town in Nebraska did not expose her to that concept. She is on a path that even she isn't aware of. I look forward to her eventual discovery as well as seeing where this path will lead her.

Stan is a messenger, struggling to deliver his message, and overcome his many illnesses. He is still as obsessed as ever with getting the message delivered. He is still struggling to discover the cause of his unsolvable illnesses.

And me...well, I'm as headstrong and ornery as ever, still finding humor in what others find to be absolutely frightening. I'm still fulfilling my role as everybody's mother, caregiver, and keeper even when they don't want me to. And, well...I'm ready to tell my story, in the hope of helping people, like me, who have struggled daily to make sense of what is happening in their lives, with or without the supernatural, paranormal, and Etherean presence.

Everything is finally okay—wonderful, in fact. Stan and I have spent so many years, wasted years, worrying about money. We have squandered precious personal energy on allowing fear to control every aspect of our lives. Fear of the Black Ops. Fear of the Ethereans. Fear of the Zetas, the Orions, the mantis people, the possum people, and the Elohim. All of which necessitated our moving seven times in six years. Our own self-judgments created a fear within us that people would've deemed us insane. Not to mention my jealousy issues, fear of losing my husband, and family. Fear of the anger that we each independently harbored. As well as frustration and fear of never having the answers to what was happening to us.

When I look back over these past ten years, I see these struggles, heartbreaks, betrayals, confusion, pain, and horrible arguments, as well as dear friendships found and lost. Yet, everything is okay. How, you might ask, do these things mean that everything is okay? Well, because I also have witnessed limitless love, great adventures, laughter, happiness, understanding, acceptance, and beauty. The constant in my life has always been love. Love, that has stood the test of time and carried me through the darkest days of my life. Like a beacon, it shines on what is most important: my family. As Grandpa, the Orion says, "Love is…love is!" Love has conquered all. It's okay. We have learned a great truth. By simply stating, "Everything will be okay, it will work itself out eventually," we have released most of the fear that has held us in a death grip for the past ten years. We have begun to think positive thoughts surrounding love, money, safety, home, family, relationships, and friendships. It may indeed be miraculous, but everything truly is okay. We have re-evaluated the true effect of the abductions—the contact that the

Orions and the Elohim have had on our lives, and we are blessed by the enlightenment that has filled our hearts and minds.

As the Elohim said, "Stan is here to…help with the transition. He is here to help others to understand that there is more. The shift will happen naturally. That's all it takes. It is very simple, but it is a daunting task."

The shift has begun, and these simple truths that I am sharing with you are part of moving ourselves into the oneness, of shifting our thoughts and feelings, and of releasing our fears. And by understanding what is really going on, who we really are, and what our true purpose is…here on Earth, we are creating the shift. In the words of my dear and amazing friend, Dannion Brinkley, *New York Times* bestselling author of the books *Saved by the Light, At Peace in the Light,* and *Secrets of the Light,* "We are great, powerful, and mighty spiritual beings of light, living in a physical world with dignity, direction, and purpose." I hope people will finally understand the message: we are not only of the oneness—we *are* the oneness!

In the process of shifting my thoughts and emotions, my ex-husband and I have established a friendship. Regardless of past hurts and blame by either of us, we now move forward with a single purpose, that of loving our children and learning from our mistakes. We chose to be together for a time in order to do something very important. Our important mission was the creation of our children, April, Nicole, and Jacob. And through them, we have achieved greatness. Our children are our legacy. Though my children are not Stan's by blood, he too has shaped their lives as their step-dad. Many times they have been angry at him for bringing the paranormal weirdness into their lives, for forcing them to question their beliefs. But, in the end, they have become such enlightened adults. Adults that are free from worrying about exploring the unusual, for believing in ghosts, ETs, and such things as energies and other realities and dimensions, free to be themselves in spite of what other people want them to believe, including Stan and I... they are free thinkers.

It has been difficult for me to accept the hybrid children as real. Or to accept that Stan and I had created a child who is part human and part something else. I recently met a child claiming to be my hybrid daughter, Suri. I did not speak to her, but she gave a stranger a message for Stan and I, which Stan shares in *Answers*. I watched this beautiful child from afar, too afraid to approach her, but knowing without a doubt who she was. Upon meeting these children face-to-face I can no longer deny the truth—they are indeed real! As you can see in the picture below, Suri is very much human in appearance, yet she is different in a beautiful way. I can't be a mother to her in the same sense that I can for April, Nicci, and Jake. But I can be a positive influence in her life by being a messenger and sharing my story, my children's story, Stan's story and Suri's story as well.

On the following page is a picture of Suri, taken at the Aztec Conference in Aztec, New Mexico; and my sketch of Kioma.

The photographs of the other girls are in Stan's third book, *Answers*.

I realize now that these beautiful Etherean star children have chosen to incarnate into this reality to help us here on Earth grow into our magnificence. I also now understand that Stan and I have chosen to be here for the same reason, to bring forth a new reality. Much the same as each and every human on this planet has chosen to be here on Earth, at this time—the bravest of the souls in God's keeping, in my opinion. We have each chosen to suffer the pains of humanity, to learn the lessons of what this existence has to teach

Suri at the Aztec Conference in Aztec, New Mexico. Photo by Lisa Romanek.

Kioma. Drawing by Lisa Romanek.

us. But most importantly, we are here to bring peace, love, and understanding back into the world. These star children—Ethereans, that I had thought were the product of rape, an abomination—turn out to be quite the opposite. They are miracles! These magnificent beings have come here now at this time to help us with a very simple but daunting task, to know and accept them for who they are. They are a part of us, and we are part of them—a much larger family than we could have ever imagined—the family that God, the oneness, created.

These miraculous beings that we call hybrids are not jaded by jealousy, anger, or any junk that parents dump in the laps of their children. They are unspoiled by human wars, hatred, greed, and fear. Without fear, these children are truly free! Without fear, their love flows from them unfettered and unconditionally.

I tell you truly, this is the bigger picture that has become abundantly clear to me. I am not a victim. I signed up for this. This single thought has changed everything. There are no accidents, there are no coincidences. These off-world beings, these Ethereans, are teaching us how to become free of fear. Fear is the opposite of love. Fear is the root of all the ills on this planet. Be free of fear and love will unfold like a lotus blossom.

This is the message—the lesson. Be fearless. Be free. Love without condition. The truth is…we are so much more than we know. We are of the oneness, the divine singularity of God, just as our star brothers and sisters are. We are love and we are loved.

As I finish this book I must tell you that I have much yet to learn. Life's challenges can still be daunting. I still get angry, I still shed tears of frustration and sorrow, and yes at times I still experience jealousy. I have not shed every ounce of fear. But I now approach them from a different perspective.

All I ask of you, my friends, all of you that have arrived at this point in time with me, is to ponder my story, our story, and consider adopting a different perspective: Keep an open mind, go forth with love, and live without judgment. Be fearless. You know who you are.

About the Author

Lisa Romanek, author of *From My Side of the Bed: Pulling Back the Covers on Extraterrestrial Contact, A Spouse's Point of View*, is the wife of well-known extraterrestrial abductee/contactee Stan Romanek.

Lisa realized that there are two sides to every story, two sides of every bed. She has learned the importance of taking that which is personal, and at times embarrassing, and turning it into that which serves the public—especially anyone who's walked in her same slippers as the spouse of an abductee.

Lisa takes you on her heart-wrenching and sometimes hilarious journey as the wife of Stan Romanek. Her courage and integrity mix well with her Nebraska-born charm and her decades of work with the elderly—all of which is reflected through the tenderness, compassion and warmth that she embodies and carries as a spokeswoman for those who feel alone in a world of extraterrestrial chaos beyond their control. As the wife of an abductee and mother of three children, Lisa has a simple message to share: Live without fear, love without limit.

25213087R00153

Made in the USA
Lexington, KY
22 August 2013